BÄRLE'S STORY

one polar bear's amazing

recovery from life

as a circus act

BÄRLE'S STORY

Else Poulsen

foreword by
G.A. BRADSHAW

GREYSTONE BOOKS
Vancouver/Berkeley

Greystone Books Ltd.
www.greystonebooks.com

Cataloguing data available from Library and Archives Canada
ISBN 978-1-926812-87-8 (pbk.)
ISBN 978-1-926812-88-5 (epub)

Editing by Nancy Flight
Copy editing by Maureen Nicholson
Cover design by Gerilee McBride
Interior design by Jennifer Griffiths
Cover photograph by Tom Roy
Photographs by Detroit Zoological Society, Kathy Jo Ferguson,
Carrie McIntyre, Betsie Meister, People for the Ethical Treatment
of Animals (PETA), Else Poulsen, and Tom Roy
Printed and bound in Canada by Friesens
Distributed in the U.S. by Publishers Group West

We gratefully acknowledge the financial support of the Canada
Council for the Arts, the British Columbia Arts Council, the
Province of British Columbia through the Book Publishing Tax
Credit, and the Government of Canada through the Canada
Book Fund for our publishing activities.

Greystone Books is committed to reducing the
consumption of old-growth forests in the books it publishes.
This book is one step toward that goal.

To Bärle

CONTENTS

FOREWORD

. Do you know what the mathematical expression is for
longing? The negative numbers. The formalization of the
feeling that you are missing something. PETER HØEG

LIFE EVOLVES MUCH like the number line. Days traverse one by
one—1, 2, 3 ... 300 —gradually accumulating into months, years,
and decades. When a loved one passes, units of time reverse from
union to separation, and while absence may blend into the fabric
of everyday life, its trace remains; a yearning lingers. The Portu-
guese call this beckoning emptiness *saudade*.

There is something of *saudade* in the story of Bärle. It is
achingly beautiful. The author brings a weaver's skill to the task
of drawing together multicolored threads of observation, experience, and science to create a dense and fascinating tale. We are
granted a rare opportunity to see a polar bear up close in ways
that no adventure tour, nature show, or visit to the zoo could
ever provide. Our privilege springs from the intimate knowledge
that Else Poulsen has absorbed over years spent in the care and
recovery of captive bears. In the unfolding of Bärle's story, we are
brought backstage, behind the scenes, from her beginnings in a
snowy arctic den to the hollow cruelty of circus and the drama

and uncertainty of rescue to her resting in salvation—still captive, but with dignity restored.

x This elegant narrative is infused with something more than keen reportage: it has an unspoken theme of love. The polar bears come alive because of the open hearts of the author and the comrades she encounters along the road. The band of bear professionals, scientists, advocates, veterinarians, and honest citizens who save Bärle represents a fragile, but formidable, frontline between polar bear extinction and survival.

The polar bear is in peril. Like other wildlife, this giant, powerful god of the North has been brought to his knees by human greed and ignorance. Juxtaposed with the horrors inflicted on Bärle and her kin, however, is the other side of humanity—a vast, compassionate potential to right the terrible wrongs that wildlife suffer.

Bärle's story is a story of the times. Our species is faced with an inescapable choice. Are we willing to sacrifice human privilege so that other animals can live their lives as we would wish for ourselves, lives of dignity and freedom? Are we willing to save and restore our own humanity? As ice sheets recede and polar wildlife is pushed into ever-shrinking fragments of habitat, we behold our own loss. The *saudade* that steals upon us while reading about Bärle is a primordial thirst for the past when the winds and waters spoke and we could hear their wisdom. It was a time when, like tribal peoples of old, we could pick cloudberries alongside ursine kin with a sense of shared joy at summer's bounty. It was a time when our hearts and those of the bears beat as one with the pulse of all nature.

Bärle beckons. We can return.

G.A. BRADSHAW

ACKNOWLEDGMENTS

THIS BOOK TOOK longer to research and write than anticipated, as Bärle's mysterious and convoluted life story revealed
itself to be full of dark twists and turns. I would like to thank my
family, Olaf and Rigmor Poulsen, Olaf and Valerie Poulsen, Ellen
Poulsen and Robert Wade, and Kristen and Rebecca Wade for
their tremendous support every step of the way. I am indebted to
Carol Bresnay, Carrie McIntyre, Ron Manseau, and Tom Roy for
their commitment to Bärle's recovery and the telling of her story.
I am grateful to the folks who have been so wonderfully help-
ful with this project, sharing information and heartfelt personal
insights. Thank you all for your time and goodwill: Lisbeth Amos,
Dorothy Avery, Mindy Babitz, Heather Bacon, Chris Bartos, Tracy
Belting, Sonja Berlin, Gay Bradshaw, Sabrina Brando, Diane Brown,
Robert and Carolyn Buchanan, Scott Carter, Wendy Chambers, Car-
ney Anne Chester, Cory Davis, Maria de Almeida, Andrew Derocher,
Ryan De Voe, Shannon Donahue, Ann Duncan, Kenneth Ekvall,
Libby Eyre, Cinzia Faiazza, Nancy Flight, Gail Ford, Jeff Gerecke,
Tony Hamilton, Vibeke Hansen, Gail Hedberg, Silke Herzberger,
Steve Herrero, Alison Hood, Ulli Joerres, Chuck Jonkel, Ron Kagan,

Ben Kilham, Lydia Kolter, Debbie Leahy, Teresa Marshal, Wayne McCrory, Betsie Meister, Tim Mengel, Brigitte Mercier, Steve Olson, Jeff Owen, Richard Patch, Jim Pissot, Jason Pratte, Sharon Prien, Holly Reed, Evelyn Reis, Doug Richardson, Una Richardson, Charlie Robbins, Birgit Rudolph, Charlie Russell, Rob Sanders, Bernd Schildger, Marion Schneider, Gordon Stenhouse, Ian Stirling, Chris Tabaka, Stacey Tabellario, Debbie Thompson, Lynn Waddell, Lisa Wathne, Diana Weinhardt, Kristin Westwood, Delcianna Winders, and Karen Wolf.

PROLOGUE

I N THE THREE years that it took me to write *Bärle's Story*, polar bears aged roughly four million years, give or take a million years. Until 2012, polar bears were thought to have diverged from brown bears who hailed from the giant cave bear early in the Pleistocene epoch, about a million years ago, but recently it has been determined that they are at least five million years old. Polar bear research is being generated fast and furiously to satisfy our insatiable appetite for information about global warming and its likely effect on the planet and its inhabitants—particularly us. Humankind's sudden interest in the well-being of wild polar bears is akin to the miners' interest in the canaries they took with them into the coal mines in the early twentieth century as detectors of methane and carbon monoxide gases. A dead bird meant immediate evacuation of the mine. Since we can't evacuate the planet yet, we have to understand what dead or compromised polar bears mean to human welfare. The human response to global warming and its effect on wild polar bears ranges from complete denial and scoffing to complete acceptance and doomsday prediction, with reasoned thinking somewhere in the middle.

The wild clash of opinions is often rooted in monetary consid-
erations. A rather chilling example of this human opportunism
is the 375 percent increase in global demand for polar bear pelts
at Canadian fur auctions between 2007 and 2012 reported by the
International Fund for Animal Welfare.

In contrast, there are polar bear biologists who were interested in polar bear well-being long before they were unwittingly
shot into superstardom by the media frenzy around global warming. There are interest groups such as Arctic Action Teams, whose
founders work day and night to help communities develop
planet-saving carbon footprint reduction programs, and there are
individuals who care enough about animal welfare to report the
use and abuse of polar bears in a blisteringly hot equatorial circus.

Bärle (pronounced "Bear-la"), a wild female polar bear whose
freedom was stolen by human greed and who suffered unimag-
inable hardship because of human ignorance, also lived to recover
from her trauma through human compassion. I was given the rare
opportunity of working with a team of altruistic people, most of
whom I had never met before and many of whom worked for organizations that are frequently adversarial, such as People for the
Ethical Treatment of Animals (PETA) and the Association of Zoos
and Aquariums (AZA). These groups put aside the human agenda
and focused exclusively on the animal agenda. In many ways the
rescue of Bärle and six other bears, who became known as the
Suarez Seven, was the result of an unchallenged movement of
goodwill and charity.

Although I tried repeatedly to contact the Suarez Brothers Circus
for their comments on the events described in this book, they did
not respond.

I was privileged to be given the task of Bärle's recovery. It was
heartbreaking, heartwarming, and heart-mending to work closely

with her, providing her with the tools she needed to express herself as a polar bear without fear of repercussion. Interviewing the other team members so many years later for this book was a remarkable experience. The goodwill that acted as the catalyst for the rescue, rehabilitation, and recovery of Bärle and the rest of the Suarez Seven is still alive today in each person whose life was touched by Bärle, Alaska, Royal, Willie, Masha, Boris, and Kenny. Bärle's story had to be told as an example of what's possible when people set aside the human agenda and focus exclusively on the animal agenda.

1

A FEDEX'D POLAR BEAR

Bärle's Arrival at the Detroit Zoo

IT WAS LATE, cold, and humid. I was tired, cold, and damp. But the weather made it a perfect November night in 2002 to be waiting for the arrival of a polar bear. Scott Carter, several other staff members, and I had brought the Detroit Zoo van to the FedEx hangar of the Detroit Metropolitan Wayne County Airport about thirty minutes early, and the plane was late. We met Debbie Leahy from People for the Ethical Treatment of Animals (PETA) and various tired media people. Everyone was just hanging around, intermittently talking to each other. As the director of Animal Welfare and Conservation, Carter met with the media. My colleagues and I spoke in snippets. We had heard that one of the male polar bears, Royal, had died en route. We were anxious. I just wanted the airplane to land, to assess Bärle's status, and to bring her home for the first time to the Detroit Zoo.

To calm our nerves, we chatted about inconsequential topics. Thinking that Dr. Ann Duncan, the Detroit Zoo's head veterinarian, might be stepping off the plane in summer pants, we had brought her a coat. That seemed funny.

When I ran out of subjects, I filled my head with nonsense. I watched the FedEx packages move along the conveyor belt, orderly, nothing falling off, no packages being kicked around by gorillas. I was impressed. FedEx truly does look after each package. I made a mental note to always use FedEx, not so much because of humane package care but because they airlifted six polar bears out of the sweltering Caribbean to their new northern homes for free.

5

Suddenly the deafening roar of air-breathing jet engines brought me back to life, and we were engulfed in a thick cloud of hot fumes and activity. FedEx staff beetled around, maneuvering mobile stairs and platform lifts to greet the giant Boeing MD-10 dragon, which had come to rest just outside the hangar door. This was its final polar bear drop-off. Blowing off the last steam, the engines finally stilled, and the side of the belly opened up. The enormous cargo door was the size of the letters *Fe* in the company name printed on the plane's port side.

It was dark outside, but the blinding lights from inside the hold shone like a godly salvation around a comparatively small crate topped with dozens of bags of dripping cube ice. Hyper-focused, I was drawn to the crate like a bug to light but was instantly reprimanded for moving toward the plane. In minutes the crate was mechanically conveyed onto the elevated platform lift and lowered to the ground, then brought into the hangar. FedEx staff and media people kept a respectful distance. Being near an adult polar bear in a wooden crate can be unnerving for laypeople, no matter how well-reinforced with metal ribbands that crate was. Bärle had arrived.

Others looked after waybills, pulled up zoo vehicles, and answered media questions. I slowly approached the metal mesh end of the crate and knelt down several feet away. I didn't want to cause Bärle any further stress. She had already suffered seventeen years of torment in the circus world, followed by a twenty-four-hour shakedown cruise in the belly of an airplane.

The small bear with raggedy fur turned around and moved right up to the mesh to face me, smiling slightly and making direct eye contact when I quietly called her name, "Bärlein." Her expression and behavior had the soft, sweet innocence of a tired cub. She caught me completely off guard. I was expecting a small bear crouched in a corner with a weary, guarded demeanor or, conversely, a small, fearful, angry bear lunging at my face. A wild bear trapped in a crate or a captive bear who hasn't been crate trained will often lunge forward in attack, jaw-snapping and spitting at the human face peering in. A severely abused bear will often shy to the back of the crate, press himself to the wall, lower his head, and take sideways glances at his human predators, jaw-snapping, drooling, and gutturally growling. Bärle was the most abused bear I had ever been assigned to work with, in both the longevity and the circumstances of her abuse. I did not understand her greeting; it seemed out of character for a bear. I gently smiled back and slowly raised my hand to touch the mesh between us in a gesture typical of both humans and bears.

In the mix of warehouse white noise, the delivery door opening and the zoo van backup alarm beeping caught my attention and interrupted our private interlude. We were on the move again. Zoo staff and I, and the now-habituated FedEx staff, moved the crate from the platform lift into the back of the van. We said our thank-yous and good-byes and drove off, commenting that the FedEx staff would have a good story to tell their families at breakfast. As we headed north on the I-94E to the zoo, we were again engulfed in darkness. Bärle was quiet in her crate, and we humans fell back into our own thoughts as we drove through the fog. It was odd that Bärle seemed neither terrified nor aggressive.

Personality in bears, as in humans, is determined by a ceaseless stewing of genetic makeup, personal life history, and the current environment. In my work I use research, deductive reasoning, and insight as tools to come to some understanding of the individual bears whom I work with. I study the bear's natural history, dig up his personal history, and assess his current environment. Only by considering these factors did Bärle's behavior make some sense to me.

Scant records suggested that Bärle was likely born in 1984 in the Canadian Arctic, was orphaned in 1985, and was possibly brought to Germany in 1986. From there she became the property of Eric Klant, who contracted out his bear show to the Mexican Suarez Brothers Circus with trainer Alfred "Fredy" Gafner in 1989. When Klant died in 1990, he willed the bears to Gafner. Sadly, animals taken from the wild in that era often have sketchy records or none at all. Even when records exist, they may have been purposely falsified to skirt conservation, welfare, or import-export laws. We were certain, however, that Bärle had been suffering in this equatorial circus for thirteen years.

Tropical Caribbean living is not for polar bears, who, over five million years, have evolved to handle extreme, frigid temperatures. The mean annual highs and lows in Puerto Rico range from the mid-seventies to the mid-eighties Fahrenheit. To put this into proper polar bear context, wild bears plodding along the frozen arctic tundra can overheat if the ambient air temperature is above minus four degrees Fahrenheit, forcing them to take cooling plunges into the frosty ocean or to lie flat on their bellies or backs on a frozen surface. Ever wonder why polar bears seemingly trudge along at a slow pace? They set their pace so as not to overheat. Animal welfare investigators and veterinarians documented temperature spikes up to 113 degrees Fahrenheit in 2001 and 2002 next to the mobile cages holding the bears at the circus.

Aside from the oppressive heat, Bärle and the other five polar bears lived with cruelty every day, without even one iota of refuge meaningful to a polar bear. People from all walks of life had reported incidents in which trainers used whips and sticks to hit the bears on the face, the head, and the hindquarters. Diana Weinhardt, the chair of the Bear Advisory Group for the Association of Zoos and Aquariums, observed the bears wince when approached by the trainer carrying a blunt fiberglass stick, indicating to her that these bears had likely been hit by that stick and possibly by that trainer to elicit some desired behavior.

Leahy, in her position as director of Captive Animal Rescue and Enforcement with PETA, visited the polar bears at the circus five times. In November 2001, she attended the show three times. It was hot, a little over eighty degrees Fahrenheit. Each time, the bears were panting, and they were filthy. The stench of urine filled the tent, and there were flies everywhere. The audience was sparse. Although Leahy had viewed videos and photographs of the bears taken by other complainants before visiting the circus, she was taken aback by the squalor. "It was horrifying. You had to see it for yourself," she said in a personal communication.[1]

In a later visit, posing as a tourist, Leahy was invited on a behind-the-scenes tour by Fredy Gafner. The bears were held in small, grimy cages. "Fredy complained that the U.S. government was telling him what to do," Leahy said. "That he had been forced to buy an air conditioner for the bears. He said the bears were difficult to get out of the air-conditioned holding area to do their shows. He also complained about the pool he was forced to purchase for the bears."[2] The pool was approximately eight feet in diameter and only four feet deep—the size of a polar bear bathtub. It was questionable whether the large males could even submerse themselves in it.

In August 2001, a United States Department of Agriculture (USDA) inspector wrote in his report, "The polar bears were in the transport vehicle for a total of approximately 55 hours at a temperature of between 79 degrees and 87.5 degrees during the daytime hours. This is outside the normal range for these mammals."[3]

Dr. Pedro E. Nunez Sepulveda, a veterinarian in Puerto Rico, had observed the bears to be "caged individually in spaces too small for their size as the lengths of their bodies were practically reaching from one end to the other." He further noted,

> They didn't have access to a pool and you could see that some bottles of drinking water were dirty with tomato, lettuce, and carrot. A large quantity of bloody diarrhea, with a lot of mucus, was draining from one of the cages, accumulating on the floor, and several flies, attracted by the apparent bad odor of the blood, were clearly visible."[4]

Bärle and Alaska, the two small females, were not even safe from their own kind. Under the imposing threat of human trainers in the performance ring, any one of the gigantic males would regularly lash out and attack a female in a sort of Stockholm syndrome behavior.

After Bärle arrived at the Detroit Metro Airport, her ambient temperature had dropped from hideously tropical to thirty-eight degrees Fahrenheit in less than twenty-four hours. Perhaps that partly accounted for her relaxed demeanor in greeting me. But thinking about Bärle's life on the road with Dante's Inferno, I realized that the only reprieve Bärle had had from her human predators was when the circus was traveling. In her crate, treated like cargo, she was safe. In her crate, she couldn't get hit or otherwise hurt by humans or male bears. Maybe that was why she was so calm. But if her crate did offer her the only refuge she had known in thirteen years, would we be able to coax her out of it and into her new quarters at the zoo's animal hospital quarantine?

10 As we pulled up to the zoo's security gates, the van flooded with artificial light. They were expecting us. The security gate always opened a bit faster, we joked, when the officer knew we had carnivores on board as opposed to birds, fish, or butterflies. We appreciated the speed; we just wanted to get on with it. When we arrived at the animal hospital, we all piled out of the caravan and put on our professional roles. We, including Bärle, were home.

Someone turned on additional lights; someone wheeled in the old gurney; someone opened the back doors of the van. When all was in place, some of us entered the belly of the van and surrounded Bärle's crate. On the count of three, we heaved and slid the crate forward toward the raised gurney. It must have weighed four hundred pounds. It didn't help that we were hunched over in the van. Again, on the count of three, slide, and again. Bärle concentrated on maintaining her balance by standing up and riding it out. She was well rehearsed in behaving like cargo. Her patience was impressive and, from my experience, oddly unbear-like. No short huffing and jaw-snapping, no long-drawn-out expulsions of air and spit, and no jabbing paw-punches at the metal mesh. On the final haul, we had to keep the heaving motion going from van to gurney. Someone lamented that we needed a hydraulic platform lift like FedEx had. Grunting, we all agreed. "On three, push!" We did it. Then, like a human conveyor belt, we wheeled the crate from the loading dock into the hospital quarantine area, where Bärle would live for the next thirty days.

The end of the crate was pushed forward to rest perpendicular to the enclosure's animal entrance door. In zoo-speak, we call these doors "slides." Operated remotely from outside, the slides are opened and closed using either a manual or a pulley system. I opened the keeper door and hopped into the enclosure. While my colleagues were chaining the crate onto the enclosure fence to secure it for Bärle's departure, I began interacting with her, hoping to illustrate that we were harmless. With bears, as with humans, it's important to make a good first impression. I take no chances by relying on personal charm; I buy my way into grace with food treats. I had grapes—sweet, juicy grapes.

I crouched in front of Bärle, and we locked eyes. Like humans, bears communicate using a combination of words, sounds that have specific meaning, and body language. If a bear wants to communicate something to another creature, he will lock eyes with that creature, unlike gorillas, for instance. For them, as I have experienced, staring is perceived as a threat or, at the very least, as rudeness. I offered Bärle a grape by holding it up to her nose through the metal mesh. Never taking her eyes off mine, she gently took the grape with her lips and then intentionally dropped it, a small smile on her lips. I have experienced this behavior before with bears whom I've had a trusting relationship with and have interpreted it as politeness. A bear may not want or need what I am offering at the time but will take it if he wants the interaction to continue. If the bear is annoyed, he will simply refuse to take the object, refuse to make eye contact, form his upper lip into a point or square, or express an escalation of other, more aggressive behaviors, such as paw-slamming and huffing.

I didn't know if Bärle had ever tasted grapes before, and since I had no history with her, I had no idea if she was being polite. We knew only that her diet in the circus had consisted largely of day-old bread, lettuce, carrots, and occasionally cheap dog food. I offered her a second grape, which she gently took with her lips and ate, keeping her eyes locked on mine. Her slight smile had not waned. It didn't matter if she ate the grapes or not; my objective was to show her that we were trustworthy so that she would feel comfortable enough to leave the crate. As long as she and I were calmly interacting, we were planting the seeds for a positive relationship. Then she broke eye contact and moved her nose closer to the grapes in my hand to smell them, the slight smile still there.

Bärle's face was a curious wash of age and youth. She was a small bear with a head no bigger than mine. Her fur was a mess. The long guard hairs were broken or missing, the undercoat was woolly and matted, and she had bald spots revealing flaky, black skin. Bärle's facial muscles had atrophied, giving her a sunken, weary appearance befitting an abused, neglected bear. She looked older than her nineteen years—not unusual for a mistreated animal—yet a cub-like innocence, a simple sweetness, and, oddly enough, trust shone through her eyes and expressions. The complexity of it all, and her radiance, drew me right in.

I continued to offer her grapes at an accelerated pace since she was now eating them with increasing vigor. Michelle Seldon, our associate curator, peered through the door and quietly told me the crate was now locked in place. "It's time."

I quickly tossed a sparse trail of grapes down the hall from the room that Bärle would step into first to the end room, where a giant, fluffed straw nest as tall as she was and twice her circumference awaited her. The grapes now took on a new significance. When bears need to consider their next step, they may feign interest in an unrelated object, giving them time to consider their options while appearing nonchalant. This is called displacement behavior. Humans do it too. If you notice that a stranger is rudely staring at you, you probably break eye contact and check your watch or cell phone or pretend to be absorbed in other things while you consider your options: fight, flight, or indifference.

As I stepped out of the enclosure, I locked and double-checked the door used by humans. We quietly lifted the slides to the enclosure and the crate. A focused silence fell over all of us; Bärle stayed seated. I stopped breathing, watched, and waited. Quietly I called her name. One ear rotated in my direction. Bärle held her nose forward; twitching its wings, she inhaled, assessing the environment. And then took a step forward. Exhaling suspense, we whispered words of encouragement: "Good girl." Then she took the next full step over the threshold and into the new enclosure. Fighting to contain our great delight so as not to frighten her, we slowly, quietly closed the slides behind her.

For us humans, this moment was deeply moving. Some staff members had tears in their eyes; we were closing the door on Bärle's torturous circus life forever. But there was no reason for Bärle to believe that this was not just the end of yet another move from circus gig to circus gig. No doubt she had detected the favorable differences, the drop in temperature, the grapes, a large enclosure, and a nest of straw so fresh you could smell its sweetness—especially if you were a very tired bear.

Bärle feigned interest in the grapes on the floor. When she moved forward, her back legs seemed stiff, a little unsteady. We would have to monitor them. Slowly, but seemingly unstoppably, she moved forward, gaining speed down the hall to the straw pile. Like a dog in the first snow of the season, she approached the pile cautiously, first mouthing, touching, smelling, saliva draining from her mouth and nares, then putting one paw in and then the next, then mowing her belly through it, and finally falling over in a full-body roll-and-rub dance, enveloping herself in the straw. With straw hanging from her brows and caught in her dreadlocked undercoat, she finally crashed onto her side and fell asleep. Like tired, relieved parents after an ordeal, we quietly turned out the lights and softly closed the door.

On my way home in the darkness, I asked myself the question that has haunted me for years: "How could anyone abuse this bear?" I have learned over time that the perpetrators are often surprised to learn that they are being accused of neglect and abuse. Neglect is an insidious form of abuse, caused by ignorance, a focus on human agendas, and sometimes pure indifference. To fully assess the extent of neglect, one has to understand how this animal is genetically programmed to live in his wild niche, and how impervious to short-term change that really is.

14

In the 2002 criminal trial in which the Puerto Rico Department of Natural and Environmental Resources brought misdemeanor cruelty charges against the Suarez Brothers Circus, Dr. Pedro E. Nunez Sepulveda testified:

> It has been stated by the Suarez Brothers Circus and their two veterinarians that these polar bears are *acclimated to the tropics* because they were born in captivity and they have traveled constantly, a few times to the tropics. I would like somebody to explain to me, how, in only 10 or 20 years, the Suarez Brothers Circus and their veterinarians have changed all the structural and functional adaptations in these bears which has taken nature—natural selection—more than 50 million years of evolution to develop for Arctic life... To presume that these animals are *acclimated to the tropics* to obtain permits and justify deficiencies in the maintenance, care, and husbandry of the polar bears represents an insult to the intelligence of any honest veterinarian, zoologist, scientist, or any person with genuine interest in wildlife.[5]

I'm certain I'm not alone in sharing Dr. Sepulveda's indignation. Unfortunately, the presiding judge did not understand or was focused on the human agenda, as he found in favor of the circus.

That lumbering polar bear on sea ice in the Arctic Ocean is as flawlessly and uncompromisingly made for that environment as a squirrel monkey is to the Amazon rain forest. The two species cannot switch places and thrive any more than you or I could live either on the sea ice or in the jungle canopy.

Thrilling, real-life technological advances in nuclear and molecular genetics—which make the laboratory tinkering in *CSI* television programs look like child's play—have enabled paleontologists to uncover many details about the origins of the polar bear. An April 2012 study, sequencing the nuclear DNA of polar bears, brown bears, and black bears, suggests that polar bears and brown bears diverged more than 600,000 years ago, much earlier than previously thought. Just before that, in 2010, mitochondrial DNA was skillfully extracted from the oldest-known polar bear fossil, discovered by Ólafur Ingólfsson in 2004 in the Svalbard Archipelago, Norway's slice of the Arctic. Charlotte Lindqvist and her team of geneticists determined that this bear and his relatives had been alive 120,000 years ago and had hybridized with the now-extinct Irish brown bear. Most recently, in July 2012, Lindqvist and an international team of scientists determined that polar bears are five million years old and that during previous periods of global warming they have interbred with brown bears living on the northern islands of the Alexander Archipelago in Alaska.

Even with modern technology, it continues to be difficult for scientists to determine the exact lineage and important evolutionary dates for polar bears because they live and die on the sea ice. The remains of most polar bears simply disappear into the ice and ocean and are churned into fodder for other life-forms, forever lost to science and discovery.

The entire evolutionary process from pre-polar bear to modern-day polar bear, which took as much as five million years, is a heck of a long time compared with the measly thirteen years that the operators of the Suarez Brothers Circus suggested their polar bears took to adapt to the tropical Caribbean. As a species, polar bears have been through numerous periods of global warming, most recently the Eemian epoch, which began some 125,000 years ago and ended about 115,000 years ago. Pockets of bear populations are thought to have survived by moving with the remaining ice sheets. In the interglacial period we live in, the Holocene epoch, it is thought that polar bears will do the same—move with the receding ice as the globe warms—until there isn't any ice left.

In 1996, on a work trip to Churchill, Manitoba, in the Canadian subarctic, I was standing on the tundra looking out to sea. It was early October, and the polar bears had gathered and were lying about and resting. Some were on their backs with one or two legs in the air, waiting for the sea ice to form over the Hudson Bay so that they could head north for another winter of seal hunting. It was forty degrees Fahrenheit, but the wind chill, humid and biting, ripped away what little heat my body generated. It felt like minus thirteen degrees Fahrenheit. In my anorak with the hood up and cinched around my face and my felt-lined Kodiak boots, I was still frozen solid! So what changes took place over five million years to allow polar bears to evolve from ancestral bears? Above all else, if you are going to live on the frozen sea ice, you have to stay warm.

Polar bears can do that. Starting from the inside out, a polar bear in good physical condition has deposits of fat hanging onto his muscles throughout most of his body, sometimes up to four to six inches thick on the rump. If the bear is in sumo shape—a four or five on the polar bear biologists' subjective Fatness Index—then the fat can even be stored between the muscles and around or in the organs. This exceptional energy reserve keeps the organs and unborn cubs insulated from the elements. But what truly keeps the bears warm is their immensely dense fur, consisting of a woolly undercoat interspersed with long guard hairs. I have found guard hairs from polar bears longer than six inches. Polar bears can have up to 14,840 hairs per square inch. In contrast, humans have on average a mere seven hundred hair follicles per square inch on their head.

The hairs on a polar bear are clear, hollow, and open like straws at the ends. The bear's body heat and the sun warm the air inside each hair so that the bear is enveloped in a blanket of millions of cozy air pockets. A polar bear's evolved ability to maintain heat energy is perfect. A wildlife biologist in the late 1900s tried to identify polar bears through infrared field photography, but they were invisible except for a tiny color blip of air as they exhaled. So a polar bear's problem is actually cooling off, which he does by leaping into the Arctic Ocean or sprawling his torso and limbs on his front or back on the sea ice or on the tundra permafrost. Clearly, to accomplish this, a bear needs an Arctic Ocean, pack ice, tundra, or at the very least a high-powered industrial chiller.

Bärle and the male bears had none of these in the circus. Their basic needs summarily neglected, they were missing not just the ability to walk, run, swim, jump, dig, and climb at will, but the ability to find a mate, raise young, hunt, and share food at will, and the ability to shut out the boiling cauldron of incessant noise, smells, and actions of their human predators. What they got was a lack of choice, physical and mental pain, and the unrelenting stress of daily survival in an environment hostile and meaningless to their polar bear sensibilities. Most people who give this even a moment's thought would understand that these bears were living in an abusive environment. "Polar bears in the tropics" is an obvious oxymoron, and yet thousands of people had watched the bears perform for nearly thirteen years and little was done. How does that happen?

Homo sapiens have compartmentalized animals according to the human agenda since our emergence on earth some 200,000 years ago. There are animals that we eat, wear, live with, trade, compete with, love, and are entertained by. Animals have been an integral part of our existence on earth since our arrival, but it hasn't been until the last twenty years that a field of scientific study called anthrozoology has been developed to help define our relationship with them. The relatively late emergence of the field tests the meaning of our Latin name, *Homo sapiens,* which may be roughly translated as "wise man." Although our relationship with animals has been a symbiotic one, it hasn't been a mutualistic, one benefiting both species. While we are heading toward a more humane relationship with the animals that we associate with, the journey itself has been a slow process as the wooden wheels intermittently grind to a halt in the ruts and rocks of culture and money.

Some individuals evolved faster than others. Leonardo da Vinci, who lived in the late 1400s, is often quoted as saying, "The time will come when men such as I will look upon the murder of animals as they now look upon the murder of men." That time has not yet come, and it is not on our radar. We are in an age of turmoil and dichotomies. Although it is culturally acceptable in North America to house a female domestic pig, an intelligent and sentient creature, in a two-foot-wide cage where she is unable to turn around or express normal behaviors and is annually required to give birth to two litters that she cannot cuddle, it is not acceptable to treat a domestic dog this way. If most of us are not comfortable with the obvious animal abuse in factory farming, we choose not to think about it but instead to believe that it is a necessary evil because, after all, we have to eat. The fact that humans have to eat does not, however, stop North Americans from scoffing at Asian cultures for eating dogs. In North America, dogs are meant for companionship and sometimes work, but not for eating. We know dogs really well and would not eat them.

Having worked closely with domestic pigs, Vietnamese potbellied pigs, wild Eurasian swine, peccaries, and warthogs, I know pigs really well and would not eat them. In my experience they are personable and highly social and at times seem more mentally dexterous than dogs.

The act of eating an animal—intelligent or not—seems to justify our killing it.

Remarkably, the we-eat-it-so-it's-okay argument is also used for polar bear hunting. The only country in the world that allows trophy hunting of polar bears is Canada. The International Union for Conservation of Nature (IUCN) Polar Bear Specialist Group (PBSG) reports that there are approximately twenty thousand to twenty-five thousand polar bears left in the wild, and two-thirds of them live in Canada. In November 2011, the Canadian government listed polar bears as a species of special concern under the Species at Risk Act. This status pales in comparison to their status as threatened under the United States Endangered Species Act, which only allows their hunting for sustenance by aboriginal Alaskans. Both of these ratings take a backseat to Norway's complete ban on polar bear hunting, which has been in effect since 1973. The British *Daily Mail* broke a story in March 2012 revealing that the I Love Hunting Club in China was to take wealthy Chinese hunters to Nunavut to trophy hunt polar bears. Although the hunt was legal under Canadian law, an international outcry embarrassed the club into withdrawing its business from aboriginal guides in Resolute, Nunavut. Among others, the Nunavut Member of Parliament Leona Aglukkaq was quoted as saying, "When any hunt takes place, including a sport hunt, the meat from the animal is used to feed community members, no usable part of the animal goes to waste."[6]

Although that argument does illustrate a level of frugal custodianship, it is dwarfed by the mountain of scientific evidence on the perils of global warming, on top of which sits the beacon of impending disaster, the polar bear. Through the lens of traditional knowledge, however, the Government of Nunavut has interpreted an increase in polar bear sightings to mean that there are more bears. But biologists interpret this phenomenon to mean that more bears are becoming landlocked for longer periods as the pack ice recedes and does not re-form in traditional habitats. Pressing the point, the Nunavut Wildlife Management Board increased its hunting quotas for polar bears in October 2011, despite the opposition of the IUCN PBSG. Completely dropping the ruse of any ethical argument, the tour operator of the I Love Hunting Club, Scott Lupien, said, "And if you believe the ice caps are melting as some claim, these bears are going to die anyway, so we may as well hunt them."[7] At this juncture, eating them or not becomes a moot point.

Animal species like black bears that reproduce well and can, to a certain extent, tolerate persistent human encroachment into their wilderness areas are often called pest animals. Thus marginalized, they are subjected to attempts to reduce their numbers either in mass culls or through irresponsible wildlife management such as the 2011 killing of 145 black bears in the Alberta tar sands. Today's pest animal easily becomes tomorrow's endangered species.

In his laissez-faire these-bears-are-going-to-die-anyway attitude, Scott Lupien has plenty of company. The price of polar bear pelts is soaring, as buyers speculate that the species will become extinct in our lifetime. According to Fur Canada, a retailer in Nanaimo, British Columbia, a ten-foot polar bear skin rug retailed for CDN$25,000 in January 2014, and the demand was so great that customers have to pay 50 percent down and be placed on a waiting list.

In Russia, the illegal killing of polar bears is soaring to new highs, and according to the IUCN the country is losing up to two hundred bears annually to poachers in the Chukotka, which is one of its four subpopulations of bears. Although hunting the bears has been illegal since 1957, the country still allows the importation of Canadian pelts which sell for USD$30,000 and this market is thought to be fueling the killing. In China, polar bear pelts are reportedly selling for US$80,000.

Topping the list of absurd animal abuse on the human agenda has to be the use of animals in media and entertainment. Seven dirty, chalk-dust-covered polar bears being forced to perform ghastly apparitions of human behaviors such as walking up stairs, dancing to music, and playing with balls while walking upright—after thirteen years—finally received enough intelligent human empathy to secure their rescue. Until that time, thousands upon thousands of people watched and either enjoyed or ignored their performance.

The thinking process that allows humans to be indifferent to or even take part in some obvious forms of animal abuse and lead otherwise moral lives is called doubling. This term was coined by Robert Lifton, the psychiatrist who wrote *The Nazi Doctors, Medical Killing and the Psychology of Genocide,* exploring the coping mechanisms of Nazi physicians who caused death and harm during the day and acted as ethical persons off the job. According to psychologist and animal trauma expert G.A. Bradshaw, doubling falls into the same category as dissociation, splitting, and numbing of one's ethical senses and allows you to "have your cake and eat it too."[8] The doctors' failed collective justification for their actions expressed in the Nuremberg Trials amounted to "I had no choice; it was my job."

Animals too have a sense of morality, of justice and fairness. According to behaviorists Marc Bekoff and Jessica Pierce, morality is about social balance. In their book *Wild Justice: The Moral Lives of Animals,* they define morality as "a suite of interrelated other-regarding behaviors that cultivate and regulate complex interactions within social groups."[9] They argue for evolutionary continuity, which identifies the differences between animals, including humans, as a matter of degree rather than kind. In other words, humans share more similarities with other mammals than just plumbing. We share additional cognitive and sentient tools that allow all of us, animal and human, to successfully negotiate our habitats on this planet. It's taken man a long time to walk down this intuitive trail.

Having a sense of fairness, how did Bärle and the other polar bears understand their own suffering? I can only guess that the abuse was such that their only objective was just to survive another day, and fairness didn't even enter into it.

2

BERRY PICKING WITH POLAR BEARS

How Bärle Ended Up in a Caribbean Circus

O N A SOUTH-FACING slope, trickles of marble-sized snowballs rolled down the hummock, again and then again, in waves from an underground disturbance. The surface rolled and jutted and finally erupted, and out popped a polar bear head. She blinked repeatedly, getting used to the sun again after eight months of little to no light. She inhaled through her nares, receiving windborne information, and exhaled through her open mouth in short gapes. It was April 1985.

In the womb of her snow den, she had given birth to twins in mid-January, as was the habit of most of the females on the west coast of the Hudson Bay. When the cubs were born, they were slightly larger than a pound of butter and weighed about the same. Delicately furred in clear, fine hair, eyes and ear canals closed, they tucked neatly into her belly fat and fur for warmth and food as they suckled on her teats. The mother was awake on and off, licking the cubs to keep them clean and dry, nudging them back in place when they sometimes wiggled or rolled away and cleaning the den by eating their feces. The beauty of nature's mechanics is that one behavior often has numerous benefits. Licking the cubs also stimulates their circulation and consequently assists in their biological development. At four weeks old, their ears opened up, and at five weeks old, their eyes fully opened.

24

In their sixth week, the cubs began to push themselves along with their legs, developing muscle, trying to walk. Their mother had already scraped out a small additional room in the packed snow, possibly because she was adjusting the den temperature or the airflow, or both, and possibly for more room. As genetically planned, it was time for a change. The cubs weighed at least twenty-two pounds, were several months old, and were wobble-walking. The den, which had been a wonderful conservator against the cold and wind and the challenges of winter's darkness, was now too small and cramped, as the cubs trampled all over their mother and each other. And they were getting cranky, sometimes wanting to feed, sometimes acting colicky and bawling. They were teething. First the incisors came in, then the canines, causing them discomfort for about a week. Finally, at eight weeks old, their premolars erupted.

The female was stretching her limbs and moving about more, feeling the need to get out and hunt. Her fat reserves were running low as she hadn't been carnivorous in eight months.

The timing of her and her cubs' new developmental needs was perfect. On the coast, the local bearded and ringed seal females were nurturing their young in birth lairs beneath the snow. By now the seal pups had grown to be 50 percent body fat and were ready for eating by hungry polar bear families.

For the next couple of days, the female polar bear poked her head in and out of the hole in the roof like a sentry, breathing in the air and assessing the environment. The exit had flooded the den with cool air and light, which the cubs likely took some getting used to. On the third day, the female fully emerged from the den for the first time since the fall. She slowly slid down the knoll about fifteen feet, spread-eagled on her belly, then rolled onto her back, wiggling in the snow to clean her fur, keeping her eyes on the den exit. In seconds, two little cub heads popped up like puppets from the crater, looking for their mother. The cubs first tried to scramble down the hill on their feet, then tumbled head over paws, rolled like balls, and finally giving up complete control, ended up in a free-fall slide right into their mother.

Over the next two weeks, the female and her cubs spent around 80 percent of their time resting in the den. When they were outside, it was always as a family. The cubs had many repetitive items on their to-do list: to play-wrestle with each other, to play-wrestle with their mother, and to play-wrestle with whatever snow, rock, tree, or bush they happened to bump into or fall on top of. When their mother began to dig with one paw through the snow to the ground vegetation below and eat it, they dug with one paw too. When their mother, suddenly alerted to a scent or noise, stood on her hind legs and sniffed and adjusted her ears, the cubs stood up on their hind legs and sniffed the wind and adjusted their ears too.

The female had her own agenda. She spent most of her time resting, watching her cubs, periodically stretching, rolling in the snow to clean her fur, or taking walks with the cubs. Throughout the day she repeatedly brought her young in and out of the den. They were small and could easily become hypothermic, but they grew quickly on their mother's milk, which offered them 30 percent milk fat and would greatly improve their chances of surviving on the sea ice, which was their destination.

Until now the family had not gone farther than three hundred feet from the den. The day before they abandoned the den completely, they spent more time outside. The next morning, they left for the sea ice. The female had dug her winter snow den right next to her fall earthen den, and they were twenty miles west of the Hudson Bay coast. It was a slow trek for the family. Every quarter of a mile or so, the female stopped and made a round saucer-like daybed in the snow large enough for her body, and she would sit or lie down to nurse and warm her cubs. Although their mother was leading the family in as straight a line as topography and safety allowed, the cubs added to their own distance by weaving in and out of that line and playing on the way, expending all kinds of energy. On occasion a tired, cold cub would get a ride on his mother's back.

Life did not get any easier when the bears arrived on the ringed seal pupping grounds. First the cubs had to learn to stay where their mother dropped them off, many yards away from the seal den. That part seemed easy enough; they could occupy their time with a rousing wrestling match, as they had at every stop on the trip there. Noisy bear cubs who announced their presence were a bonus for a seal mother, who would disappear lightning fast from the lair into the water with her pup, if the pup was old enough. If not, she was forced to leave the pup behind. Even in good seal pupping years, polar bears were successful in their hunt fewer than one out of every ten attempts. It was hard for the bear cubs to be quiet, especially during their mother's first unsuccessful hunting attempts, when one can assume they had no idea what she was doing. And sitting there at a distance to watch her as she watched and listened to the snowy ground didn't hold their attention long. Rowdy behavior received a serious disapproving look from their mother, and sometimes she was forced to return to them to restore decorum.

The cubs suddenly became interested in their mother's snow-staring behavior when in a flash she crashed through the snow with her front paws and pulled out an edible seal pup. It would be many months before these cubs were heavy enough to successfully slam their torsos through the snow to catch seal pups, never mind full-grown seals in their lair. An adult ringed seal is smaller than other seal species, but 150 pounds of seal is still a lot when you are a polar bear cub weighing 50 pounds or less. Their other food source, the bearded seal, can grow to be 500 to 800 pounds. Hunting them is a job for seriously large, experienced male polar bears, not goofy little cubs. In the meantime, their job was to watch and learn. When you are an excitable first-year cub, it's also tempting to try to get paws-on experience and repeatedly thwart the objective.

Hunting grew easier as the snow melted with the onset of summer, leaving only ice. At this time of year, when the seals haul out onto the sea ice for rest and air, they are exposed to predators. The cubs could watch and smell both prey and hunter, as their mother demonstrated different hunting techniques. Here the cubs could hone their skills, which were becoming formidable with size and age. They followed and learned life skills from their mother until her attention drifted to male bears and breeding and they were expelled from her company.

Bärle's life could have begun this way, but we don't know what happened in the first years of her life. It's thought that Bärle was born and raised by her mother on the west bank of Hudson Bay in 1984. The 1980s were highly productive years for the Hudson Bay polar bears. Most females in that area had twins, some had singletons, and a few had triplets, which is unusual today. Many females weaned their cubs after the first year. These yearling cubs struck out on their own, possibly because the food resources were plentiful and the cubs had rapidly gained weight. Bärle could have been one of those lone yearlings and may have become ensnared in conflict with humans. She could have been one of the yearlings whom the Government of Manitoba sent to the Ruhr Zoo in Germany in 1985 as a trouble bear. Her sibling might have died during the summer of the first year, leaving her on her own. In the 1980s, a full 38 percent of yearling cubs died out on the open ice during their summer hunts. Being a polar bear cub is a very dangerous business.

It's also possible that Bärle's mother was purposely shot by a poacher and the orphaned cubs were sold to the captive wildlife entertainment industry. This sort of thing happened with great frequency in the early 1900s but had become illegal and was considered unethical by the 1980s, forcing the business underground. Such events still occur today, though less frequently.

For at least forty thousand years, humans have lived with polar bears in the Arctic, competing for the same food sources and alternately being preyed on by or preying on each other. The settlement of Churchill, Manitoba, was accidentally established in 1931 on a polar bear migration route and is today world renowned as the polar bear capital of Canada. There is a certain integrity in living peaceably with bears in polar bear country. It's dangerous for both species, and responsible people and bears stay alive. Both humans and polar bears make daily risk-management decisions about actions to take to live normal lives in their environment.

It is a common misconception that the arctic tundra is a barren wasteland with minimal biodiversity. In a convolution of natural events, berry-picking season, goose-hunting season, and polar bear off-ice season all occur from August to October. The nutrient-rich tundra heaths produce at least fifteen varieties of wild berries, including blueberries and crowberries, cranberries, gooseberries, buffalo berries, and cloudberries. Local people and bears alike take advantage of all of this bounty, but it can be a tricky game of mutual avoidance. Jeanne Reimer, owner and operator of the Seal River Heritage Lodge, talks about berry picking with polar bears:

Dymond Lake is a favorite place for the bears to congregate...
We scope out which berry patches are actively being used by
bears and then go to other ones, or sometimes if the bears are at
a distance we just pick until one or two of them come too close,
then we leave... Most bears try to avoid you, except for some
young male bears... They seem to need to have the older males
knock some sense into them.[1]

When hunted wild geese are cleaned outside the lodge, the remains
are thrown into a "gut pile" to attract the bears in the area. While
the bears are busy eating discarded goose parts, Reimer and her
companions can go to the berry patches to pick with their husky
dogs. Most berry bushes reach somewhere between one's ankles
and one's knees. Crouching down and bending over to pick berries
leaves a person in an extremely vulnerable position, and so berry
picking with an armed friend who is the designated guard is common practice, much as a designated driver is common practice in
urban communities.

At the Seal River near the lodge, cloudberries grow in great
numbers. They look like peach-colored raspberries and are related
to them. Once a member of a film crew visiting the Churchill
area to record daily life asked Reimer if polar bears eat cloudberries. Having never observed such behavior, she said, "Not that I
know of." The following week the camera crew filmed polar bears
picking cloudberries. Reimer laughed and commented, "You just
never know!"

Lynn and Gord Martens, owners of the Bears' Den Bed and
Breakfast in Churchill, went mussel picking on the coast one day.
The tide was out, exposing rich beds of bivalves on the beach. Up
on the rocks behind them they noticed movement. A polar bear
who was lying on the rocks and looking in their direction raised

his head and inhaled the air, seeking information. Then he lowered his head again and continued resting and sunning himself. Mussel picking recommenced, Marten's firearm slung across his back.

In summer, geese and polar bears congregate in the Akimiski Island Migratory Bird Sanctuary in James Bay, close to the west coast of Hudson Bay. The geese are there to breed, lay eggs, and eat berries. The polar bears are there to oversummer, and they eat the berries, the eggs, and the geese. One summer, Lydia Lefebvre was banding wild snow geese and Canada geese in the sanctuary with the Ontario Ministry of Natural Resources. Biologists and their technicians take human and bear safety seriously. The camp was surrounded by fencing, foods were stored properly, and wastes were processed accordingly. The helicopter, the most important piece of equipment on the island, because lives depended on its ability to operate in an emergency, was surrounded by hot wire, electric fencing, to add further security.

Although a designated guard always carried a firearm, bears were scared away from bird banders on the tundra using bear bangers and rubber bullets, and occasionally the pilot would fire up the chopper's engines to run off the more persistent. Care was taken to not follow bears when the chopper was airborne, because they can suffer from heat exhaustion when running. Staff members who considered a polar bear in camp a photo opportunity were considered a liability and did not last long on the job.

Even with all of the safety precautions in place, researchers remained sensitized and alert. It was very early morning. Everyone in camp was sleeping. Lefebvre was having an odd dream: a polar bear materialized out of the rolling fog and moved toward her. She awoke immediately. She pulled on her anorak and boots and went outside to see if all was well. "I'm not really sure why I felt I should check the grounds based on a dream, but I just did it," she told me.

She moved around the corner of the building and came face-to-face with a polar bear staring back at her. Lydia sounded the alarm and woke the others, and the bear was scared off. It's possible that the bear was going to try to break through the fence. 31

Not all encounters with polar bears end peaceably for humans, but fatalities are rare. In Canada between 1965 and 1985, nineteen people suffered injuries in polar bear encounters and only five of them died. Roughly two-thirds of the world's polar bears live in Canada. From 1900 to 1985, no deaths and only one injury related to a polar bear attack were reported in Alaska. Although more humans worldwide have been encroaching on polar bear habitat since 2000, the number of deaths seems to be even lower. The only recent death on record is that of Horatio Chapple, a seventeen-year-old boy who was killed by a polar bear on August 5, 2011, while camping with a group of young adults at Von Postbreen glacier on Spitsbergen Island in the Norwegian Svalbard Archipelago. Bear biologist Tom Smith stated, "I have had people say that polar bears are the most dangerous bear in the world—yet these numbers suggest something else. Sure, they are large and well equipped to kill prey, but I do not believe it is their inclination to seek and kill humans as is often said."[2] As Jeanne Reimer, Lynn and Gord Martens, and Lydia Lefebvre and her colleagues all demonstrated, one has to respect the nature of the bears to live well with them.

In contrast, the killing of female bears to generate orphaned cubs for the entertainment industry suggests moral bankruptcy. In 1996, Ken and Sherri Gigliotti, from Winnipeg, Manitoba, observed seven polar bears beaten with rods to perform at the Suarez Brothers Circus in Cozumel, Mexico. The bears were later identified as Bärle (Bärlein), Kenny (Kenneth), Royal, Boris, Willie (Wilhelm), Masha, and Alaska. The Gigliottis were enthusiastically told that three of them—Bärle, Kenny, and Royal—were from Manitoba.

When the photographs from the circus pamphlet that the Gigliottis brought back home were published in the *Winnipeg Free Press*,
there was an international public outcry. At that time it was estimated that approximately thirty wild polar bears had been given
to zoos around the world, many of them substandard, through
Manitoba's Polar Bear Export Program, and their stories were
made public. Bears who were deemed by government officials to
be a problem because they were routinely attracted to human food
sources and bear cubs orphaned by the hunting industry were considered for relocation, euthanasia, or export to zoos.

Zoocheck Canada, alerted to a possible bear welfare issue by
the Winnipeg Humane Society in early 1995, was already research-
ing the inner workings of Manitoba's Polar Bear Export Program
when news of the bears in the Suarez Brothers Circus hit the global
fan in 1996. Since Manitoba government records were difficult to
come by and arrived only piecemeal after three arduous requests
through the Freedom of Information and Protection of Privacy Act,
Zoocheck launched its own fact-finding mission, assisted by animal welfare experts around the world. Bears were found to have
been shipped to tropical and subtropical locations such as the
Chapultepec Zoo in Mexico City, Jardim Zoológico de Lisboa in
Portugal, and the Taipei City Zoo in Taiwan, among other locations.
Zoocheck Canada uncovered the possible shipping in 1985 of three
orphaned polar bear cubs to the Ruhr Zoo in Gelsenkirchen. In
interviews, zoo staff told Ingrid Pollak, founder of the Vancouver
Humane Society, that the zoo had received in 1985 one female and
two male cubs, along with two adult bears. The cubs and adults
were sold and shipped in 1986 to new owners. The adults were sold
to the Zoo Am Meer in Bremerhaven, Germany. No one seemed to
know where the cubs were sent, though it was suggested to Pollak
that they might have gone to the United Arab Emirates.

The Ruhr Zoo was no ordinary zoo. It was a family business that had been operating on City of Gelsenkirchen land since 1949, and it acted more like an international clearinghouse trading in wildlife than a reputable zoo. PETA obtained a copy of the export permits issued by the Canadian Convention on International Trade of Endangered Species of Wild Fauna and Flora (CITES), which confirmed the export in 1985 of three polar bear cubs from Manitoba to the Ruhr Zoo. One permit identified as Man. 079 was clearly issued for two polar bear cubs, but the document had been tampered with. Some of the document has been typed, but a handwritten note identifies the female cub as Bärle, and an additional note in another person's handwriting identifies a single male as being both Royal and Kenneth. It's impossible today to ascertain who wrote what, when, and for what reasons. Another permit identified as Man. 078 was issued for two adult bears and a second female cub on the same dates. Two things are certain, however. First, the Government of Manitoba does not refer to wildlife by personal names. Individual animals are given numbers. Second, bears who were candidates for the Polar Bear Export Program were routinely tattooed on the upper-right lip. No tattoos have been identified on Bärle, Kenny, or Royal at the time of the rescue or since.

These points suggest that if Bärle, Kenny, and Royal came from Canada in 1985, they might have done so by illegal means. They may have come from Manitoba, but could just as easily have come from Ontario, Quebec, Labrador, or northern Canada in poach-and-nab operations involving the purposeful killing of female polar bears with young to generate orphaned cubs for the zoos, circuses, and entertainment. To add to the confusion, the bears could have come illegally from any other country where polar bears are indigenous, including the United States, Norway, Greenland, and the former Soviet Union. There is no shortage of bad guys in the illicit acquisition of and trade in polar bears. Paper trails are a quagmire of fraud, deceit, and fanciful explanations. In fact, Alaska, the only other female polar bear in the Suarez Brothers Circus, was traveling under a false identity. The circus identified her as a bear previously named Snowball, who was born at Zoo Atlanta in 1983, sold to exotic animal dealer Fred Zeehandelaar in 1986, and then resold to Zoo Rostock in Germany. Terry Maple, director of Zoo Atlanta, gave public proof that Alaska was not Snowball by noting that Snowball had died at Zoo Rostock in 1994 at the age of eleven.

While the first three years of Alaska's life remain a mystery, her suffering at the circus was well documented. In June 2001, the USDA reported that she had several brown patchy areas on her face, thought to be a fungal infection that had not been addressed by the veterinarian. In August, an anonymous animal welfare investigator reported that Alaska was in a deteriorating condition. She had no hair left on her face, a discharge from her right eye and nose, and difficulty holding up her head.

Thanks to the valuable information that Maple was able to provide, because record keeping for zoo animals had greatly improved over the years, Alaska was rescued. She was confiscated from the circus on March 6, 2002, in Puerto Rico by staff from the United States Marshals Service and the United States Fish and Wildlife Service. Alaska was given a home at the Maryland Zoo in Baltimore, where she surprised the keepers by being the calmest bear they had ever worked with. Loud mechanical or sudden noises seemingly made no impression on her. She also slept for an unusually long time when given the reversal for her anesthetic during her first full veterinary checkup at the zoo, snoozing through the noise of mechanical doors operating and staff gently calling her name.

Early in Alaska's recovery, it dawned on Chris Bartos, the assistant animal curator, that Alaska might be deaf. Before presenting this theory to her colleagues, Bartos conducted a behavioral test by unceremoniously slamming a metal grain shovel into a metal door so that it reverberated throughout the dens. Alaska was sleeping and showed no response. To convince herself that the bear was still alive, Bartos poked Alaska gently with a stick. The bear woke and looked wearily over her shoulder at Bartos as if to indicate that she just wanted to finish her nap. The veterinary team at the zoo called in audiologists from the Johns Hopkins Hospital to give Alaska the BAER (pronounced "bear") test—probably the first time the test had ever been given to an actual bear. The acronym BAER stands for Brainstem Auditory Evoked Response, a test that is frequently used to assess hearing ability in dogs and humans. Alaska was immobilized, and electrodes were attached to the skin on various areas around her head. Like a television antenna detecting signals, these electrodes detect electrical impulses in the cochleas and auditory pathways in the brain. "Alaska's printout was flatlined," stated Bartos. "She was completely deaf."[3]

It is difficult enough to imagine the day-to-day struggle of a polar bear living in the tropics and being physically and mentally tormented in a circus environment. Adding deafness to those challenges would suggest nearing a psychological tipping point. But Alaska coped. Her survival strategy became clear when she was introduced to Magnet, the zoo's fourteen-year-old single male polar bear. Magnet had introduced himself by shoving sticks and straw underneath their shared door before he had met her. He was either giving her gifts, which male bears do, using the items as an olfactory calling card, or simply doing it to share bedding. There was no ruse; he was excited to have her around. On the day of their introduction, Alaska punched him in the shoulder a few times to make him back up, which he did, and they became inseparable after that. To her last day, Alaska did what Magnet did, whether he was playing, going indoors, going outdoors, eating, or resting. He had become her hearing aid.

Meanwhile, Kenny's personal history is only slightly less convoluted. If he did go to the Ruhr Zoo as a cub in 1986, he may
have been sold to a circus in 1987. But then the trail grows cold
for twelve years. Kenny resurfaced in November 1999, when he
and Boris were mentioned in an article in the British newspaper *The Independent*. According to the article, Kenny and Boris
had been working for Ursula Böttcher in the State Circus of the
German Republic.

In its heyday, some of the East German circus acts traveled the
world. Böttcher, a tiny woman standing only five feet tall, either
had nerves of steel or was an adrenaline junkie, since she trained
up to fourteen polar bears at one time. When these gigantic bears
stood on their hind legs, they towered over her by another five
feet. Böttcher's signature shtick was that selected bears would lean
down and kiss her on the lips at the end of the show, a finale aptly
named the Kiss of Death. This act delighted audiences in Europe,
North America, and Asia from 1973 to 1998. Böttcher's livelihood
caused her numerous personal injuries and the death of at least
one colleague, but she survived to retire in 1998 after the reunification of the two Germanys. With the dissolution of the state
circus and the growing awareness of animal welfare concerns,
circus performers found it more and more difficult to earn a living
in Europe.

Böttcher, who did not actually own the bears, had hoped
to place them at the Rio Safari Park near Alicante in Spain. An
accountant named Kurt-Christian Knischewski was hired to sell
all of the circus assets, including the animals. He found it difficult
to sell Kenny and Boris, who were eventually the only two animals left. The bears had been castrated, and at that time zoos only
wanted bears who could be bred. To this day the Rio Safari Park
exhibits animal acts, suggesting that the polar bears might have
been slated to entertain there as well. Knischewski found a home

for them at the Madrid Zoo, but both zoos were controversial, with most critics citing Spain's subtropical weather as a problem. As journalist Imre Karacs wrote, "So just what do you do with a polar bear who needs a new home? The idea of sending a 1,500 lb. furry beast designed for the Arctic Circle to a city where the summer temperature can hit 50° C [122 degrees Fahrenheit] seems at best bizarre, at worst cruel."[4]

Against Böttcher's wishes, the bears were said to have been sold to zoos in Germany. Records seem to indicate that Kenny and Boris were in fact sold to Zoo Valkenburg in Holland, thought to be the surreptitious name for the private animal collection of Eric Klant, the circus performer. Klant's act was hired by the Mexican Suarez Brothers Circus in 1998, and so began Kenny's and Boris's lives touring the tropical Caribbean, where animal welfare sensibilities were not yet well honed.

Boris is thought to have been born in 1985 at the Rostock Zoo in Germany and was sold to the State Circus of the German Republic in 1987. Kenny and Boris likely arrived at the circus together as subadults. Upon their rescue from the Suarez Brothers Circus in 2002, the bears were kept together and moved to the Point Defiance Zoo in Tacoma, Washington.

They arrived at the zoo in poor condition; their fur was dirty and patchy, and they had skin abrasions and little muscle development. At first neither bear was particularly responsive to staff, but Kenny, who was said to have been Ursula Böttcher's favorite bear, seemed more responsive to shorter women. Kenny died on April 18, 2012, at the advanced age of twenty-seven years.

Royal, the third bear thought to be of Canadian origin, shares an equally murky history. From his possible shipment to the Ruhr Zoo in 1986, like Bärle, he too disappeared for years after he was reported to have been sold to an unnamed circus in 1987. Royal and Bärle reappeared years later, in 2000, in the Suarez Brothers

Circus records. Where they were for thirteen years is a mystery. It is assumed that they came to the circus with trainer Fredy Gafner from Germany in 1989. To everyone's dismay, Royal died during the rescue on November 5, 2002.

In all fairness, the Government of Manitoba was simply caught with its pants down. The Polar Bear Export Program was developed by well-meaning provincial biologists, conservation officers, and legislators to give polar bears who had come into contact with human habitats a shot at a life rather than being killed. Since human irresponsibility was at the root of bear troubles, it seemed only right to find an alternative. Gordon Graham, legislative specialist with the Manitoba Wildlife Conservation Branch, commented that "we're not interested in seeing these bears end up in circuses. It doesn't fit with our expectations of where these bears should be going."[5] The revelation that the poorly managed Polar Bear Export Program was also causing tremendous suffering to Canadian bears in tropical zoos launched the government into action. Even though it was questionable whether Bärle, Royal, and Kenny were of Canadian origin, the government began rewriting the Polar Bear Protection Act. The revision was completed in 1999 and legislated in August 2002.

The act spells out minimum bear husbandry requirements for facilities that wish to receive wild polar bears from Manitoba. In the 1990s, when the standards were first developed, they were considered to be state of the art. But they also seemed to be unattainable goals and caused a stir in the zoo industry. The rather minimalistic standard of the time was the United States Animal Welfare Act, which deemed it necessary for two captive polar bears to have a minuscule and tormenting four hundred square feet. This amounts to less than 1 percent of an acre. This requirement has not been changed.

Today the Manitoba standards are no longer blazing trails but have fallen behind the modern husbandry requirements of other governments and organizations. For instance, the act requires that one or two polar bears be housed in at least fifty-four hundred square feet. That is less than 13 percent of an acre. If there are more than two polar bears, the enclosure must be sixteen hundred square feet larger per additional bear. That is less than an additional 4 percent of an acre.

In comparison, the Government of Sweden now legislates that all polar bears be held in outdoor enclosures that are at least sixteen thousand square feet, which is 37 percent of an acre, and that they contain climbing structures. Bears that are housed singly must live in enclosures of at least eleven thousand square feet, or 25 percent of an acre. Not everyone agrees that even these standards are appropriate for polar bears. In a personal communication, zoologist Kenneth Ekvall of Orsa Bear Park in Sweden states,

> Of course nobody in their right mind would be near these minimum standards here in Scandinavia if they were to build a new polar bear facility, I hope—we have a lot of data on bad facilities and correlation of poor breeding and high levels of stereotypic behaviors. To my mind, the Scandinavian Animal Park and the Orsa Bear Park show the future of how to keep polar bears in zoos, and hopefully this will influence the design of future enclosures and be a turning point.[6]

Both of those facilities measure their polar bear enclosures in hectares.

Although the Government of Manitoba now needs to rethink, revise, and re-legislate the Polar Bear Protection Act, when it was legislated it far surpassed the actions of other governments and organizations; Manitoba beat the governments of both Canada and the United States in polar bear conservation protection. In February 2008, Manitoba designated polar bears as threatened under the Endangered Species Act, and they were listed as protected under the Wildlife Act. The United States declared the bears threatened in May 2008, under the Endangered Species Act. Belatedly, on November 10, 2011, Canada's environment minister, the Honourable Peter Kent, saw fit to declare polar bears only a paltry Species of Concern under the Species at Risk Act.

Willie's and Masha's personal histories are also fraught with discrepancies. They are both said to have been captive born at Zoo Valkenburg in Holland in 1985, but others believe that Willie was mother-raised at the Copenhagen Zoo and Masha was born at Zoo Objed in Moscow. Both bears disappeared off the radar and resurfaced years later, in 1998, at the Suarez Brothers Circus. Both bears were rescued by the North Carolina Zoo, and despite their similar history of suffering as entertainers in circus acts, they are said to have had very different personalities. Willie was laid-back, attentive, and interactive with zookeepers, while Masha was a reserved and reclusive bear who did not interact with humans.

Willie had a large dorsal hump on his nose that suggested it had been broken at some point. He was also said to have swiped at his trainer and was declawed for his efforts. Masha joined forces with another traumatized bear, attacking and killing a small female bear in the troupe. When Masha died in June 2007, his necropsy revealed that he had likely suffered incomprehensible pain over the years from a broken vertebrae that had malformed in the healing process. Masha's veterinarian, Ryan De Voe, suspected that Masha was either hit hard on his back with an implement when he was younger or had fractured his back crashing to the ground on the slide the bears were forced to go down. In a personal communication, De Voe commented, "I've always imagined that sliding down that slide would create a pretty big jolt to the spine at the bottom, especially for an animal that weighed over a thousand pounds."[7]

All seven polar bears—Bärle, Kenny, Royal, Boris, Willie, Masha, and Alaska—were rescued from the circus in 2002 by a solid team of political opponents.

3

THE RESCUE

A Solid Team of Political Opponents

JEFF OWEN WALKED up to the curtainsider cargo hold of the circus's semitrailer truck and was attacked. The air was alive with hundreds, maybe thousands, of jumping fleas that had been feasting on the bears, and now him. He felt dozens of sharp pin-prick bites, the hair on his legs offering no protection from their bloodsucking guerrilla tactics. First item on the to-do list would be to exterminate those fleas.

Two weeks before the rescue, in early November 2002, Owen and Tim Mengel, both experienced bear keepers from the North Carolina Zoo, had been sent to Puerto Rico to stabilize the bears. The Suarez Brothers Circus had abandoned the polar bears and two workers in Yabucoa, Puerto Rico.

Owen simply wasn't prepared for what he saw; the bears' condition was much worse than he had expected. "It was the worst thing I had ever seen,"[1] he said. The semitrailer had been divided into six barred metal cages, one after the other in a line. Each bear was warehoused in a sixty-four-square-foot jail with two barred sides facing other bears' cages and two barred sides forming the walls of the trailer. Except for the two bears occupying the first and last cages, the bears had no privacy. The males had to lie diagonally if they wanted to rest on their bellies, curl up into a C shape to lie on their sides, or put their feet up against the wall if they wanted to lie on their backs. Little Bärle, who was less than five feet long from nose to rump, was the only bear who could lie down without contorting herself.

Sweat streaming down Owen's body, he next became aware of the annoying flies attracted by foul odors that sounded like faltering engines as they hopped from weepy sores to rotting food to runny feces and puddles of urine and then onto Owen's face. Sidestepping the flies, he became aware of placing his foot in soft feces, which oozed over his shoe. Some bears ceaselessly swayed their heads and shoulders from side to side, seemingly entranced, while others rested on their backs, exposing their arm and leg pits and panting. In Owen's words, "It was horrific."[2]

The trailer had been left in a field, in a makeshift compound surrounded by an eight-foot chain link fence with tattered privacy slats. A double-peaked, blue-and-white-striped, six-thousand-square-foot high-top circus tent towered above the perimeter fence. The entire installation appeared absurdly out of place surrounded by the beauty of the hills of the San Lorenzo Batholith.

For a few hours each day, the two bear caretakers, who had been abandoned with the bears, brought each bear from his or her trailer cage through a portable barred corral into the tent area. There the bears were allowed to move about freely, but they didn't. These tormented bears spread themselves out equidistant from each other and stayed there, eerily quiet, until it was time to go back into their trailer cage. On occasion they would roll on the dirt floor and stretch out. The USDA had mandated the circus to provide what was an insufficient, tiny aboveground pool in the tent. The pool may have been regulation size, but it was ludicrously small and fit only one and a half male bears. So it amounted to a bear bathtub. But it was the only body of water they had except for a pan of drinking water in each trailer cage.

The only two bears who interacted were Willie and Royal, who generally stayed within reach of each other and frequently tried to cram themselves into the pool at the same time. Later, Owen and Mengel added a second pool. The only other item in the tent was a large blue ball that the bears had been trained to balance on with all four legs. Not one bear chose to interact with it.

Owen and Mengel had to get to work. Their job was to immediately improve the lives of the bears by identifying and addressing the most critical issues related to their physical health. With the exception of Royal, the bears had lackluster coats. Their long guard hairs were missing over most of their bodies. The specialized, even longer, guard hairs that mature males have on the back of their front legs as a secondary sex characteristic had fallen out, were broken, or had not developed. There were bald spots revealing flaky black skin and open festering sores in which flies had laid their eggs. Despite their physical training to do circus tricks, the bears suffered from serious muscle atrophy. Except for Royal, they also appeared to have dental issues. Willie had broken, decaying teeth, and some were completely missing. Later he would have endodontic surgery as part of his recovery at the North Carolina Zoo.

Owen and Mengel immediately set up a new husbandry routine to address the disease-causing parasite and insect infestations. They worked closely with a local Puerto Rican veterinarian who was deeply committed to improving the lives of these animals. He and his wife or an assistant came to the compound several times a day to prescribe, administer, and monitor medications to combat the fleas and internal parasites, such as worms and protozoa. Along with rejuvenating medicines, they brought bread and jars of peanut butter. On site they slapped together dozens of drug-laden peanut butter sandwiches and fed them to the bears. Some bears ate them but others didn't, so Owen and Mengel bought two cases of human baby food at the local grocery store and concocted a baby food and medicine slurry. That worked.

Open sores and hot spots were disinfected and treated with sprays until they could be further treated after the rescue. The veterinarian also began an extensive vaccination program against numerous diseases, including rat-bite fever, which could be transmitted not only by the rats but also by the feral dogs and cats running around. To further combat the fly infestation, cleanliness became the order of the day. Cage floors and bars, pools, equipment, and food and water trays were cleaned and disinfected many times a day. Throughout the day the filthy bears were given cooling showers from hoses, which they thoroughly enjoyed.

The bears also had to get onto a more suitable diet to help rebuild their bodies. In the circus, the bears were fed bread, lettuce, apples, and carrots, and, on occasion, low-quality dog pellets. Owen and Mengel introduced meat and fish into this diet to slowly prepare their digestive system for a polar bear diet. At first the bears were not interested in fish or meats, and the transition took many months for some of them. At the compound, little by little, day after day, the brown bears turned whiter, the flea population dwindled, the flies became manageable, and feces began to take form.

Through it all the bears remained strangely aloof with humans. According to Owen, "These bears just did not warm up to you."[3] Although they accepted the positive changes, moved well from the trailer to the tent and back again, and increased their time in the pools, they did not respond to Owen and Mengel, to the veterinarian and his staff, or to their longtime caretakers.

The caretakers from the circus were perhaps in their late fifties. They had likely worked with Fredy Gafner and the bears in

Germany and immigrated with the entourage to Mexico, thirteen years earlier. Now they lived in a tiny run-down shack of a mobile home parked behind the bears' trailer in the compound. Both men spoke German and some Spanish; one spoke some English. The extent of their formal education and their knowledge of proper bear care were minimal. Like the bears, these men could have benefited from better living conditions, a proper diet, and health care. They were attached to the bears, and their futures were uncertain after the rescue. To add to their problems, it was rumored that the circus had left with their passports. Owen summed it up: "I felt bad for them; they were good people. They had very little but gave it all for the bears. With the bears' rescue, these men were now homeless and had no job. I hope something good came their way."[4]

In the years that led up to Owen and Mengel's arrival, Debbie Leahy, in her position as director of Captive Animal Rescue and Enforcement with PETA, had been tracking and investigating the circus and advocating for the bears' rescue. PETA and the Association of Zoos and Aquariums (AZA) were receiving a growing number of complaints from the public. In early 2001, PETA had appealed to the Bush administration to oppose the Suarez Brothers Circus's entrance into Puerto Rico, a U.S. protectorate operating under American laws. Robert Mattlin, executive director of the U.S. Marine Mammal Commission, supported PETA's position and wrote to the U.S. Fish and Wildlife Service: "It is the Commission's view that the maintenance of polar animals in outdoor tropical environments can be potentially injurious to such animals' health and well-being."[5] Regardless, the U.S. Fish and Wildlife Service issued an import permit to the circus for seven polar bears based on photographs of the bears' condition rather than doing an inspection. This one misguided act, however, was a turning point and led to the bears' rescue.

On one of her November 2001 visits to the circus, Leahy posed as the tourist wife of a businessman. She was carrying a copy of *Circus Report,* a newsletter of circus reviews written by circus enthusiasts. Leahy commented to circus officials that she would be back for the evening show so that she could write a review. Upon her return, she was given VIP treatment and ushered to a seat in the front row of the ring. Clowns and circus performers came and bowed deeply to her at the beginning of their performances. The bears entered the arena. Leahy remembers:

It was extremely humid. Inside the circus tent was like an oven with a strong urine stench. Members of the audience were perspiring and wiping their faces. Starting at about 6:00 PM mosquitoes were abundant and biting people in the audience.

When Alaska entered the ring, a polar bear left his pedestal and viciously attacked her—biting, clawing, snarling, and wrestling. This polar bear was the one who sat directly to Alaska's left during the show. [Fredy] Gafner broke up the fight, and as the attacking polar bear returned to his pedestal, another polar bear on the other side of the ring left his pedestal and viciously attacked Alaska, also biting, clawing, snarling, and wrestling. The polar bear sitting on her left swatted and snarled at her again while he was at the top of the slide and she was climbing the stairs.

Two bears had light-colored diarrhea that blended in with the saw dust on the arena floor. I observed Gafner using an antenna and two solid, pointed fiberglass sticks.

Gafner seemed somewhat restrained in his discipline, probably because he believed I was writing a review of the circus.

The polar bears were not cooperating, and Gafner seemed frustrated. When one bear refused to go down the slide, he climbed the steps and pushed her. Gafner looked angry that the polar bears were not responding to his commands and nudging. As soon as the bears left the ring, Gafner, with an irate expression on his face, exited the ring through the arena fence door (a temporary fence erected only for the polar bear act) and went backstage. He was gone for eighteen seconds. I could hear smashing and rattling that sounded like Gafner was beating the bears through the tunnel cage that was used for the polar bears to walk from their cage to the arena. When Gafner returned, he completed his act, which involved forcing the black bear to go down the slide backward and walk upright.[6]

On her next visit, circus management now suspected that Leahy worked for PETA, and they refused to sell her a ticket. At the ticket booth, the attendant directed her attention to a handwritten sign in Spanish taped to the window. Leahy said that she did not read Spanish. A manager promptly appeared and translated it for her, saying that the circus reserved the right to not sell tickets to whomever they pleased. Surprised but undaunted, Leahy flagged down a police cruiser that happened by and attempted to make a complaint. The officer did not speak English, but asked Leahy to follow him in her car to the police station, where she could speak to the captain, who did understand English. Leahy explained that she felt the circus was discriminating against her for her beliefs about the welfare of the bears. The captain took her complaint seriously and summoned the circus manager, whom Leahy believed to be a Suarez family member, to the police station. The manager was furious and ranted about Leahy and the situation to the captain. Nothing came of the complaint, but Leahy felt better knowing that she hadn't just walked away from the challenge at the ticket booth.

For several years Leahy devoted herself to advocating for the bears. "While it was hard work," she said, "this was one of those campaigns where everyone instantly got it, everyone understood that polar bears in the tropics was not a good idea." Leahy inspired government and community leaders, and entertainers including Canadian stars Pamela Anderson and Sarah McLachlan, Scottish star Ewan McGregor, and Mexican recording artist Patricia Manterola to speak on the bears' behalf. Directors and veterinarians from the Detroit, Knoxville, Atlanta, and Baltimore zoos, and the AZA wrote letters on the bears' behalf. In early 2002, United States Congressman Earl Blumenauer from Oregon introduced an unprecedented bill barring the use of polar bears in traveling shows and circuses, a bill that was sponsored by a bipartisan group of over 110 representatives and senators. The bill was never enacted. At about the same time, in February 2002, a court drama was playing out in Puerto Rico. On behalf of the Puerto Rico Department of Natural and Environmental Resources, District Attorney Benjamin Miranda in Ponce had filed misdemeanor cruelty charges against the circus for its treatment of the polar bears. Dr. Ann Duncan, in her position as chief veterinarian from the Detroit Zoo, was sent down to help Attorney Miranda as an expert witness. Her task was to illustrate that polar bears suffer in tropical climates. This had never been done before in a court and was not an easy task, especially since the professional opinion of veterinarians had been compromised by one or several veterinarians in the circus's employ who had testified that these polar bears had acclimated to the searing heat. Duncan had to prove scientifically that they had not.

Humans sweat, sometimes profusely, to stay cool, but bears do not. Like dogs, bears have very few active sweat glands and so must maintain their body temperature through behavioral means.

Instinctively, they pant to cool off, but panting has its limitations. As Duncan explained in court, to take the respiration rate of a bear, you count the number of times per minute he breathes in and out. Then you count the number of times he breathes in and out while panting in the heat. The hotter it is, the greater the rate of panting, but there is a cap on the number of times a bear can pant in one minute. So the bear supplements panting with behavioral changes such as moving into the shade; exposing body parts with less fur, such as arm and leg pits; or diving into a body of cool water. If the bear is unable to do these things, he overheats and may die, much the same as a dog would if left in a parked car on a hot day.

Duncan showed the court a video of the polar bears in the circus panting in the tropical heat and told those in attendance how to calculate the bears' respiratory rate. The videographer panned the camera over to a wristwatch that showed the date, time, and temperature. Duncan cited references from the veterinary literature defining the normal respiratory rate for a polar bear, demonstrating that the circus bears were in extreme heat distress. Later Duncan explained to a journalist,

> In my research, I'd discovered that a normal respiration rate for a polar bear is somewhere between ten and thirty breaths per minute, with thirty being the high end after exertion. The rate for the bear on the video turned out to be sixty while lying still. It was clear that the breathing rate was so high because the bear was sweltering. It [the bear] was actually panting.[7]

In court she further explained that a bear left to overheat and pant furiously would become dehydrated at a rapid rate and would need to replace that water, which wasn't always available in proper amounts. The bear would exhibit appetite loss from the heat and would lose weight because of all of the work he had to do just to pant.

Duncan was quoted as saying, "The cross-examination went really well. But to me, the point that we had to 'prove' seemed so obvious, that I felt it was like having to prove that gravity exists."[8] It was a shock to all when the judge found in favor of the circus, and it was over. Duncan said, "It seemed like a gross miscarriage of justice, and it was very disappointing. For me, that made their rescue just that much more satisfying."[9]

Less than two weeks later, on March 6, 2002, United States Marshals and representatives from the U.S. Fish and Wildlife Service confiscated Alaska from the circus at gun point.

Zoo Atlanta had been able to verify that Alaska had been misrepresented as its bear Snowball, effectively proving bear identity theft. Government organizations devised a secret rescue plan with Diana Weinhardt, the Bear Advisory Group Chairperson for the AZA. American Airlines had offered to fly Alaska out of Puerto Rico to Baltimore, Maryland, at no charge. Weinhardt booked passage for one lion, a zookeeper, and a veterinarian. They could not run the risk of booking passage for a polar bear from Puerto Rico because the only polar bears on the island were in the circus and the information might somehow find its way there. Just the top administrators at American Airlines were aware that Alaska was moving. With deadpan humor, Weinhardt said, "We chose a lion because we were 'lyin.' Captive lions are common around the world and moving one would not raise any suspicion. They are also a larger animal and we had to choose a species of comparable size to a small polar bear."[10]

It was a difficult time to be making clandestine travel plans in the United States. This work came only five months after the catastrophic acts of terrorism on September 11, 2001. American

Airlines, whose airplanes had been hijacked as flying bombs and who had suffered so much as a company, was now trying to create a new operations normal which included increased safety measures to guard against precisely this: misrepresentations of intent by passengers. The flight manifesto would be changed from lion to polar bear by an American Airlines executive once Alaska was secured.

The rescue team consisted of Weinhardt; Michael Briggs, veterinarian at the Brookfield Zoo in Chicago, Illinois; Christine Bartos, assistant mammal curator at the Maryland Zoo; a United States attorney general; an agent from the U.S. Fish and Wildlife Service; and numerous U.S. marshals. The marshals were in charge of securing the site during the morning raid. Again with deadpan humor, Weinhardt told the story:

> Briggs and I were in the refrigerated truck carrying the empty bear crate. When we arrived at the circus grounds in numerous vehicles, a marshal told us to stay in the truck and duck down because they didn't know if there would be gunfire. They'd come back to give us the all clear when they had secured the place. I thought, Briggs is a big guy. I'll just hide behind him. From the truck we heard lots of yelling and screaming, the clanging of metal bars, and drama.[11]

The marshals returned and told Weinhardt and the team that the circus staff was agitated and unhappy, and she was instructed to get the bear out of there as soon as possible. This was easier said than done.

Alaska was in her cage in the trailer. The likelihood of her cooperating with strangers on short notice did not seem good. To expedite matters, Weinhardt asked the two bear caretakers from the circus how to move Alaska from her cage to the crate. Apparently the men had been ordered by their bosses not to assist with the confiscation but they did anyway, likely because they cared about Alaska. The men moved Alaska from her cage, through the portable barred corral, and into the crate. The minute the bear was safely in custody in the truck, the team left the grounds and Weinhardt called American Airlines to have them change the flight manifesto. Like magic, the lion became a polar bear on her way to a new life at the Maryland Zoo in Baltimore. A few months later, back home in Texas, Weinhardt received a call from one of the other island nations. The official told her that the Suarez Brothers Circus wished to bring the polar bears there, and asked was there anything they should take into consideration. Weinhardt clearly detailed the safety risks to unsuspecting circus visitors and the population at large if there was an escape, which seemed likely since few safety protocols were being practiced by the circus. With her deadpan humor, she asked, "What's the biggest gun you have? Can you handle an escape?" The official reconsidered giving permission.

With mounting pressure from interest groups, complaints from the public, daily visits from USDA inspectors, and the likelihood that their permit request to the U.S. Fish and Wildlife Service to move the bears out of Puerto Rico would be denied, the circus chose to abandon the polar bears and their caretakers so the show could go on. The circus was said to have moved to Antigua. On November 5, 2002, the U.S. Fish and Wildlife Service officially seized custody of the bears.

Eight months after Alaska's rescue, on November 18, 2002, Owen and Mengel got up before the sun, which didn't rise over Yabucoa until 6:30 AM. They had a lot to accomplish on this, the bears' last day in Puerto Rico. It was over; their two-week reprieve to help the bears become travel worthy for the last big move of their lives was up. Emotions ran high. Expediency was critical. They had to pack the bags of six polar bears to catch a FedEx flight from San Juan at one the following morning. There was an air of finality. Weinhardt had flown in again for the last time. She showed the two bear caretakers photos of Alaska in her new home with her new mate, Magnet. The caretakers were delighted and wanted to have their photograph taken with Weinhardt. And there was an air of new beginnings. Leahy, from PETA, arrived to witness the fruits of her years of labor become reality.

As usual, Owen and Mengel worked with the caretakers to follow the bears' normal daily routine of cleaning and being moved into the tent for a time. The bears were not fed, because that evening each bear would be anesthetized for a veterinary exam before the flight and the doctors did not want to risk aspiration of gut contents into the bears' lungs. Owen and Mengel organized, checked, and rechecked the necessary tools, chains, ropes, locks, and crates that had just arrived from mainland American zoos. All day they discussed contingency plans for every juncture of the primary plan should problems arise. In a rescue operation of this magnitude, problems would naturally arise as a matter of course, since innumerable factors could not be controlled. It had been raining for days, and the compound had turned to mud. Owen and Mengel were concerned.

Late in the afternoon they went back to their hotel, ate, packed, and met their colleagues. The veterinarians who would assist with the rescue had arrived. Duncan had returned from Detroit, Dr. Holly Reed came in from the Point Defiance Zoo in Tacoma, Washington, and Dr. Gale Ford came down from the Grizzly and Wolf Discovery Center in West Yellowstone in Montana. They were also joined by Jorge Picon, who was the U.S. Fish and

Wildlife Service law enforcement agent in charge, and by Special Agent Eddie McKissick.

The airplane that Ford and a marshal were traveling on had arrived later than expected. They were now in a hurry. Ford had a handbag full of Telazol, in the form of a white powder, to anesthetize the bears for their veterinary checkup. At the airport, the marshal spotted a narcotic detection dog and his officer. Possession and transport of the Telazol by a veterinarian was legal, but being stopped would waste time they didn't have in the operation. The marshal quickly changed their course and avoided the detection team.

Once assembled, the team went to the compound to make the final preparations for transit. It was still raining, and the muddy conditions were getting worse by the minute. Fortunately, someone had thought to include the U.S. Navy Seabees in the plan, and they had brought along a serious four-wheel-drive tractor that was able to immediately extricate the polar bears' semitrailer from the mud. Around 9:00 PM the convoy was on the move with their precious cargo and headed for the Luis Muñoz Marín International Airport in San Juan, about forty miles down the road. Reed remarked, "I saw the two caretakers cry when we were pulling out. They really cared about those bears. One of them said that the bears were his kids."[12]

One hour later, the caravan pulled up to the FedEx hangar. Sadly, for security reasons, Leahy, whose advocacy work had been instrumental in securing the rescue of the polar bears, was not allowed to follow the semitrailer into the hangar, because she was not deemed integral to the veterinary and crating work that was about to take place. Leahy understood, and waited outside. Inside the hangar, the zoo professionals got busy. They had six polar bears to anesthetize so they could do health checks. The procedure was routine for the zookeepers and veterinarians alike. What was unusual was to have to do it six times in one session.

56   Each veterinarian handled two bears. Owen led the team of staff who removed the sleeping bears from their cages. He was the first one to enter the cage after the veterinarian had determined that the anesthetic had taken effect and it was safe to do so. Of the five male bears, the smallest weighed a thousand pounds and the largest, Boris, weighed twelve hundred pounds. "Oh my gosh, they were big," said Duncan. "I climbed up to try to help lift a bear. I lifted and nothing happened. You know that feeling where you know you are doing nothing but taking up space? I thought, I'm not even gonna try, so I got out of the way."[13] Owen, Mengel, FedEx staff, and Seabees formed the lifting team. Even so, it took eight full-grown men to move a male bear.

Once a bear was on the ground, the veterinarians took over. Duncan said,

> We did an examination that included an eye exam, ear exam, dental and oral exams, and skin, hair, and coat exams. We measured the rectal temperature during the procedure, listened to the heart sounds and lung sounds, and monitored the respiratory and heart rates. We palpated the abdominal cavity, examined and palpated all of the extremities, checked the range of motion on the joints, and examined the foot pads, nails, and external genitalia.[14]

When the bears were safely at their new homes, a complete blood workup would be done, including blood count, serum chemistry, serum bank, and serum titers for diseases of concern because of the bears' history with the circus. In addition, they would be tested for external parasites and internal fecal parasites.

Mengel led the team that was placing the bears in their travel crates and monitored their recovery from the anesthetic. When the veterinarians were satisfied that each bear had fully recovered, the FedEx staff weighed the crate with the bear in it and loaded the airplane.

The flight departed San Juan at 1:00 AM on November 19, 2002. Most of the staff had been up for more than twenty-four hours. Weinhardt and Ford traveled with the bears to the Memphis International Airport, which is the hub for FedEx, and Owen and the other staff traveled together on a commercial flight. In Memphis the bears would be reloaded into FedEx airplanes heading toward their final destination. Bärle was bound for Detroit, traveling with Duncan, and Boris and Kenny were heading for Tacoma, with Reed and Ford. Mengel, who was an animal management supervisor at the North Carolina Zoo, traveled directly from San Juan to the Charlotte Douglas International Airport, North Carolina, to be on the receiving end when Willie, Masha, and Royal arrived with Owen. This nightmarish planning challenge had been meticulously orchestrated by Weinhardt.

The five-hour flight to Memphis started out as routinely as a flight carrying six polar bears could. Weinhardt and Ford repeatedly checked on the bears in the cargo hold, and the bears appeared to be doing well. Several hours into the flight, however, there was a problem; Royal appeared to be sleeping. They tried to wake him by poking him gently and then tried to annoy him into consciousness by tickling his nasal cavity with a small object. Neither method worked. They thought that he might have fallen back into unconsciousness induced by anesthetic narcosis. Ford stayed in the hold with Royal, and Weinhardt went to the cockpit to ask the pilots to alert Memphis and ask them to meet the flight with a medical team. Staff at the Memphis Zoo were aware that six polar bears were coming through Memphis and were already on standby. By the time the flight reached Memphis, it was clear that Royal had died. Royal's body was transported to the zoo, where a necropsy determined that the cause of death was overheating.

When my colleagues and I arrived for work at the Detroit Zoo at 7:00 AM, Michelle Seldon greeted us with the news that we had lost Royal. It was heartbreaking. There was an impromptu silence, and then we got back to work to prepare for Bärle's arrival later in the day.

We were expecting to pick her up at the Detroit International Airport around noon. We had prepared the zoo cargo van for the transport, and we were bringing the passenger van for the staff who were assisting. Sometime into the morning, we heard that Bärle and Duncan were going to be late. FedEx had discovered that the airplane and crew that had been designated for this trip would be over their allowable flight time as determined by the International Air Transport Association regulations, so a different airplane and flight crew had to be found.

There weren't any preparations left to make to bring Bärle home, so my staff and I continued on with our regular duties. By midafternoon we heard that Bärle and Duncan would be arriving around 9:00 PM. In the early evening, we heard that Kenny and Boris had arrived safely in Tacoma. That was a relief. Later we heard that Willie and Masha had made it safely to Charlotte. I imagined that the comfort they must have felt at the zoo to finally receive their bears was shrouded in sadness because they couldn't welcome Royal too.

By midnight we were sharing in the joy. Bärle was home, safe and sleeping in a clean bed of straw bigger than she was.

4

THE ROAD TO RECOVERY

Bärle's Quarantine

THE NOTES FOR Bärle's first two days of recovery in quarantine at the Detroit Zoo animal hospital are short. Bärle slept most of the time. She would wake for a few minutes, lift her head, and then fall back to sleep. Several times she got up unsteadily to take a drink of water from the stock tank and then slowly walked back to her fresh straw nest and continued to sleep. There were no feces to remove and no mess to straighten up. She did not eat or interact with anything or anyone; she just slept. Not only was Bärle sleeping off the effects of the anesthetic and of traveling for over twenty-four hours, but she was also beginning the process of healing from thirteen years of substandard circus living.

Bärle was in ward four of the old animal hospital. In typical 1950s zoo architecture, there was a row of three barred rooms with an adjoining hall at the back, all on a cement floor raised several feet off the ground to accommodate drainage. The zoo has since built a state-of-the-art animal hospital, which opened in 2004. Bärle occupied the entire apartment of rooms, which gave her approximately 720 square feet. Under normal circumstances, a living space of 720 square feet is far too small for a healthy adult polar bear with a life to live, but it was perfect for Bärle's recovery plan. She had just spent most of the last thirteen years confined in a cage no bigger than sixty-four square feet, and we did not want to overwhelm her with too many new experiences all at once.

Bears who have been so grievously deprived and understimulated for years must be slowly acclimated to a more complex living environment. At the Animals Asia Foundation Moon Bear Rescue centers in China and Vietnam, bear husbandry experts rehabilitate traumatized bears rescued from the bear bile-farming industry in Asia. In a personal communication, Dr. Jill Robinson, founder of the Animals Asia Foundation, stated:

> Bears that lie in agony in cages, suffering pain and behavioral deprivation for years, are physical and psychological shells of the animals they are meant to be.
>
> On bear farms across Asia, they are systematically tortured for their bile through catheters, needles or permanently open wounds in their abdomen and suffer chronic infection and pain. Their teeth and paw tips are hacked away, their eyes diseased and blind, their bodies skeletal, and their limbs missing from being illegally trapped in the wild. These miserable creatures have received no free access to food or water, have struggled to move within unrelenting bars that confine them for years, and have enjoyed absolutely no quality of life at all. On arrival at our sanctuary they are fearful of people, angry, scared, psychotic, and sadly described as our "broken bears."
>
> The astonishing thing about these animals is their will to survive and their ability to recover. Gradually nursed back to health, the complexity of their environment is then slowly increased, with careful additions of ever-changing enrichment, play, and feeding regimes, which stimulate their behavioral and spatial repertoire and allow them to express natural characteristics and behaviors observed in the wild.

Carefully introduced to other bears, and released into semi-natural grassy enclosures, these previously deprived animals see their fears subside and their confidence grow as they begin to enjoy a new world of stimulus, physical activity, and social interaction with newfound friends. It is why we are here and indescribable to witness how simple acts such as foraging, playing, and, yes, having fun, can literally change a hopeless life into one that has meaning at last.[1]

We would allow Bärle to acclimate to her new surroundings at her own pace, from small to large, simple to complex, and insular to social. Circus life had stolen her freedom to make even the most basic decisions, such as what to do, where to go, when, and with whom. We would provide options for her befitting her needs as an adult polar bear as we understood them and respectfully restored her right to make bear decisions based on her own bear agenda. My colleague Scott Carter coined the phrase "What Bärle wants, Bärle gets," which aptly described our recovery plan. It was our job to provide a nurturing environment where it was safe to learn, safe to try new things, safe to fail, and safe to try again.

Waiting for Bärle was a 170,000-gallon, thirteen-foot-deep saltwater pool, a thirty-thousand-gallon freshwater pool with live trout, a grassy tundra enclosure with an outdoor cave, and a pack ice enclosure with scattered woodchip beds, a stream, and live seals of various species as neighbors. This new facility, called the Arctic Ring of Life (ARL), had just been completed in 2001, the year before. It was already inhabited by a community of seven self-confident polar bears, each of whom had a personal agenda and an opinion about Bärle's place and inclusion. For now, Bärle was to stay in her quarantine facility for thirty days. During this time she would be monitored throughout the day by veterinary staff and zookeepers. Routine tests for disease, parasites, and physical and mental wellness would be conducted. It would be a lot to negotiate, and Bärle would need a friend to help her through the process.

On Bärle's third day of recovery, I continued my work developing what I hoped would become a trusting relationship that could support her in the challenges that lay ahead. We'd made a good first impression with each other, me with my grapes and her with her gentle demeanor. I greeted Bärle in the morning with a handful of grapes. She was lying in her straw nest with her back to me. I quietly called her name several times, but there was no response. Although I knew that this was normal behavior for an abused animal, I still wondered whether she had hearing problems, was not fully awake, or had been called by another name in the circus.

I had once assisted with the recovery of a female Siberian tiger who came in with a registered name, but her previous caretakers had called her Bitch Kitty. The meager one-page report that accompanied her stated that she got along well with other tigers but not with humans, a statement that spoke volumes about her previous caretakers. Roaring, spitting, and baring her teeth whenever we entered the building, she would race to body-slam the bars until her face bled. Logically, I knew I was safe, but instinctively, all the hairs on my body stood up and every fiber of my being told me that I was under attack. Her anger at my human predecessors was so disorienting that I had to stand outside the door to fully gather my professional wits about me before entering. She had clearly been severely abused and was defending herself. We respectfully renamed her Teykova after a small river in Russia and began work on her healing.

Animals who have experienced only the predatory side of human nature often do not respond when humans call them by name. What would be the point? If human attention frequently brings hardship and pain, then the best course of action might be inaction. My guess is that Bärle was waiting for a clue about my intentions before responding. Her expectations would be based on her past experiences. Would I get angry and be abusive? Would I just feed her a treat, laugh, and leave, chattering wildly with another human, as circus patrons did?

I called her name a third time, and her ear swiveled in my direction. On the inside I was doing a happy dance; on the outside I was more controlled. I quietly showered her with praise and grapes: "Good girl, Bärle, such a good girl." I didn't want to scare her with raucous displays of emotion. I called her name again. She opened her eyes and looked at me. I gave her more grapes and more praise. The next day, she responded to my calling by turning her head. Every new day brought progress, and I was delighted.

The day after, she came over to me—by crawling on her elbows. My heart sank. This was completely unexpected and so odd. We had observed her walking, albeit with some slight limping, suggesting soreness in her hindquarters. I rewarded her with warm praise and grapes as if nothing was wrong. In all of the years that I had worked with bears, I had only observed an adult bear crawl once before, and she was attempting to crawl underneath a pair of breeding bears to investigate what they were doing. I worried that Bärle might have some form of episodic muscle weakness or lameness and reported it immediately to the veterinary staff. We carefully monitored her movements. In retrospect it occurred to me that Bärle's circus cage had been so small that moving over to the fence had been best accomplished by crawling or scooching. Here Bärle had a greater distance to cover, and crawling would be both uncomfortable and time-consuming. She must have come to the same conclusion, because she stopped crawling and began to walk over to me.

Bärle was not eating well. She had been accustomed to eating bread, lettuce, carrots, tomatoes, and on occasion, poor-quality dog food. It was remarkable that she and the other bears could exist at all on such substandard fare. This diet must have affected her development and health, and those problems would be realized over time. For now, she clearly needed help.

It was difficult to know why she wasn't eating. Was it because she had no appetite, had medical issues, or did not recognize the foods as edible, or was it a combination of all of these factors? As with our other bears, we offered her foods more than three times a day. The first meal of the day was given as soon as the keeper arrived in the morning, around seven thirty. We gave her Mazuri polar bear chow, plus a great variety of fruits and vegetables, insects, meats, and fish. Because polar bears require a combination of nutrients particular to their species, Mazuri makes a special food for them.

It is important that bears in captivity be satiated as early as possible in the morning because hungry bears will pace in anticipation of the next meal. Adult bears are genetically programmed to get food for themselves and sometimes for other bears in their company like cubs or mates. If bears are dependent upon having food brought to them, then food gathering is out of their control. This is bound to cause frustration and stress. If there is still a normal cause-and-effect relationship between the pacing behavior and the stressor, then hungry bears will pace because they are frustrated by their inability to do something about their own hunger. Severely deprived bears frequently pace all day long because the behavior has divorced itself from the initial stressors. In this case the presence or absence of food or other stressors has very little effect on the bears' overall pacing habit. In her circus cage, Bärle paced most of the day—three steps forward and three steps backward, complete with a rhythmic head swing, and a little half step at either end of the routine. We had no idea if Bärle's habit still had a cause-and-effect trigger, or if she simply paced because there was an obsessive-compulsive quality about it. We absolutely did not want to risk the resurgence of Bärle's deeply entrenched pacing habit.

Bears tend to get up with the sun. It is preferable to give bears enough food the day before so that there are leftovers to keep them occupied until the keeper arrives the next morning. Our polar bears would consume half of their daily diet in the morning. The other half of the diet would be divided into two meals, one given at midday and the other in the late afternoon. In between those meals the bears received additional occupational foods in activities known as enrichment events, such as scattering and hiding their foods, to allow them to express their normal investigative and food-retrieval behaviors. Bärle ate very little. To slowly work new foods into her diet, we first added bread and lettuce, which we knew she recognized and might eat. Bärle was as innocent as a bear cub and as far as we knew had little or no experience in trying new foods.

In circus life, bears have no opportunity to interact with other bears in a natural way, resulting in an inability to develop mature adult behavior. They become island bears, physically and socially isolating themselves from other bears. Without a nurturing, encouraging environment, it is difficult for them to overcome this insular approach to the world around them. Bear cubs have a genetic expectation that their mother will take them around their habitat and show them what's edible, what's not edible, and how to retrieve and prepare their food for consumption. That and the fact that bears communicate ideas to each other using a combination of sounds and physical demonstration gave me the idea that Bärle might allow me to show her the ropes in her new environment. Perhaps I could prime her appetite by involving her in food-eating lessons. It might also help to establish my credibility as a friend if I gave good advice about food.

I was already spending much of the day just hanging out with Bärle, bonding. Since I was another living creature, it should make sense to Bärle that I would also need to eat. To begin, I brought along bread and lettuce for Bärle and me. She understood that these were edible, and at the moment it was all she wanted to eat except for grapes. She was interested in the fact that I was eating in front of her and came over to have a closer look. I ripped half a piece of white bread off with my teeth and ate it. I held the other half between the bars for her. Maintaining eye contact, she gently took it with her lips and dropped it. It seemed she was being courteous. I repeated the demonstration. This time she took her share and ate it. I was ecstatic; this might work. I praised her softly. "Good girl, Bärle. Such a good girl." I carried on with lettuce and had similar success.

The following day I began with bread and lettuce and added peanuts to the repertoire. Since I had already been doing feeding demonstrations with a young recovering American black bear cub named Miggy, I had already learned how to shell a peanut in my mouth and spit out the shell without touching it. But Bärle simply ate the whole thing, nut and shell, and seemed to enjoy them. The problem was that the other bears shelled the nut in their mouths and spit out the shell, and Miggy had taught me that bears are quite intolerant of unbear-like behavior. She had bitten me numerous times for doing things the wrong way and then demonstrated the proper bear way to do it. I guessed it might be good for Bärle to know how to eat peanuts the bear way.

I demonstrated the technique for her, putting a peanut in my mouth, shelling it, and then pushing the shell onto my lips and blowing it onto the floor. Locking her eyes to mine, Bärle watched intently. She took the next peanut that I gave her with her lips. She seemed to fumble around inside her mouth for some time, and then out popped the shell which rested on her lips. I was excited. Keeping my eyes locked to hers, I demonstrated blowing. Without changing her facial expression, Bärle continued to lock eyes with me as the shell dried up and just fell off her lips. So I started over with a fresh peanut and this time exaggerated blowing the shell off my lips. Bärle caught on to the concept, and before long she was eating peanuts like our resident polar bears.

We moved onto other foods. Demonstrations of fruit, vegetable, and nut eating went seamlessly, but insects, fish, and meat posed a problem. I was not keen on demonstrating the delights and techniques of eating live mealworms, raw meat, or whole fish. As it turned out, mealworms wiggled and caught Bärle's attention. With a little smile on her face, she seemed amused by their movement and simply stippled them off the floor with her tongue when they stopped.

It was vital, however, that Bärle develop an appetite for raw fish, since it would become the mainstay of her diet once she was integrated into the bear community. We had many delicious species for her to choose from. She could have fresh trout that we raised from fingerlings ourselves, herring, mackerel, capelin, or any other species that I could purchase at Farmer Jack's market down the street. I had thought of eating a cooked fish in front of her, but fish made my stomach queasy at the best of times.

When Bärle came over to sit with me at the fence, I placed several dead fish at her feet. I had stuck one through the mesh and wiggled it to see if that was of interest to her. It was, but not enough for her to eat it. She just kept looking at me with a little smile on her face.

Desperate, I feigned a fish-eating demonstration by holding a dead herring up to my mouth while pretending to eat. Although that occasionally works for a human mother trying to entice her baby to eat pureed prunes, it didn't work for me. I repeatedly dropped the slippery fish onto the floor and finally down my shirt sleeve. Bärle moved her nose to my sleeve and looked into my eyes as if to let me know that that's where the cold little carcass had gone, in case I had missed it.

On another day, as luck would have it, one of the live trout that I had placed in her stock tank jumped out of the water and landed on the floor. The poor fish leapt around gasping for breath. That caught Bärle's attention. She lay down like a sphinx and watched until the fish lay still; then she touched him with her nose and he flopped around again. She had a broad smile on her face. I was anxious for her to just eat the fish and put him out of his misery, but she didn't. She sat up and tried to pick up the fish with her front paws, but he slipped out and flopped onto the floor again. When she finally did get him in her grasp, my hopes of a swift ending for him were crushed as she gingerly stripped bits of skin off the animal with her teeth. Finally she bit him in half and ate him. At this point I was more relieved that the ordeal was over than thrilled that Bärle had actually eaten a fish. After this incident, she began to eat fish regularly, dead or alive, but still not enough to sustain an adult polar bear.

I had been through appetite loss before with bears and had learned that when all else fails, go get a rotisserie chicken at the supermarket. It's a rare bear (and shopper) who doesn't salivate at the scent of seasoned roasted chicken. Bärle smelled the chicken coming as I walked into ward four, and she met the chicken and me at the fence, drooling. A bear's primary sense is his sense of smell, and I have found that if you can appeal to that sense, you can often prime his appetite. I hand-fed her the chicken through the mesh, first the drumsticks, then the rest in handfuls of meat crammed through the bars. As with her first fish experience, Bärle used her teeth to carefully remove any chicken skin that might be hanging onto the meat and dropped it onto the floor. It was an interesting yet odd behavior, since wild polar bears are known to eat the skin off of seal carcasses. Well, this was not a seal, we were not in the Arctic, and she had her reasons. Regardless, the roast chicken approach worked, Bärle's appetite improved, and so did her desire to explore and experience her new environment.

Since her arrival, she had not interacted with many of the items in her enclosure. Things had been eerily clean, orderly, and untouched. As she approached a more normal caloric intake for a female polar bear of her size, her activity levels increased in spurts. One morning about two weeks into her recovery, I knew that we were heading in the right direction when I walked into ward four and found that everything that wasn't fastened down either was in her stock tank water or had been in her stock tank water at some point overnight. There was straw everywhere mixed with water, feces, food, urine, toys, boxes, and feeders. It was a delightful mess that I was only too happy to clean up so that she could start the discovery process all over again.

For enrichment, we scattered food about the rooms so that she could go on a daily scavenger hunt. She had a belly feeder, which was a large white, fifty-five-gallon, plastic barrel with a 1½-foot-diameter hole cut into its belly. Every day the feeder was stuffed with straw or other material, such as wood wool, hay, or crumpled newspaper, and then tiny treats like raisins, peanuts, sunflower seeds, Cheerios, and Rice Krispies were mixed in. Bears spend a great deal of time rooting through the material to find and eat the treats. Bärle also received what we called lunch bags and lunch boxes, which are puzzle feeders that operate on the same principle as the belly feeder and were filled with inedible material hiding tiny food items preferred by the bear.

Bärle had manipulable items such as a brown ball, which was twelve inches in diameter, and a fifteen-inch-high brown spool, both made of sturdy plastic that she could play with or try to destroy, whichever suited her.

Bärle's stock tank held about 150 gallons of water but wasn't big enough for her to bathe in properly. We had wanted to set up a shower with a gentle spray but reluctantly had to admit that the drainage couldn't handle it properly. The cement floor would be soaked, and Bärle wouldn't have any dry land. Full-fledged bathing would just have to wait until she was moved to the Arctic Ring of Life. Apparently, though, a bear could still have water fun by cramming everything in the enclosure into the stock tank.

It was fascinating to watch Bärle experience the daylights out of objects and new foods. I had it on good authority that eggplant was relatively worthless. Two female polar bears whom I had worked with at the Calgary Zoo, Misty and Snowball, both intensely disliked eggplant. Snowball ignored it, would eat around it, step over it, and on occasion poop on top of it. Misty found that if you jumped on the fat middle of it with your front paws in the traditional polar bear ice-breaking maneuver, you could blow both ends off the vegetable at the same time and ruthlessly flatten it dead. Some of the resident bears at the Detroit Zoo had fewer problems with eggplant, but it did not make it onto their top ten lists of preferred foods.

In trying new foods, Bärle, like other bears, often sensed the items before she ate them. For fun I gave her the biggest, puffiest hollow eggplant I could find. She looked at it, then moved forward and batted it slightly with her right paw pad, perhaps to get some sense of its weight. It rolled sideways. She tongue-checked it by quickly touching it with the tip of her tongue and then lip-checked it by rapidly touching it with her lips. Suddenly, at lightning speed,

70

she stomped it into the ground with her left paw pad. Never taking her eyes off it, she bit off a small piece, sat back, and as in the fish- and chicken-eating episodes, began to gingerly strip the skin off with her front teeth. Over time she had a buildup of drying egg- plant skin stuck to her lips. Finally, she bit off a minuscule piece, perhaps for tasting, and, gaping face down, unceremoniously let it drop out of her mouth as if it were hideous. From then on eggplant was delisted as a food and placed into the toy category.

In between bouts of discovery and play, Bärle slept for hours at any time throughout the day. Sometimes, like a cub, she napped on top of toys or enrichment items; other times she went to bed in her straw nest. There were likely many reasons for her napping. Her body could have been recovering physically from so many years of substandard living and acclimating to new temperatures, foods, and medications. In addition, her brain could have been growing new dendritic material and developing synaptic occlu- sions to accommodate all of the information from new sensations and experiences that suddenly needed processing. Dendrites are a part of nerve cells that receive information from neighboring cells. Animals raised in healthy, complex environments have been found to have larger brains with more dendritic branching than those of their counterparts living in substandard, depleted environments. Animals that move from simplistic to complex environments may go through a period of brain growth.

A colleague who had studied the effects on baboons of moving from living singly in laboratory cages to living in social groupings in large enclosures shared an interesting anecdote at a conference about environmental enrichment. The researchers had expected to observe varied and active behavior in the new enclosures, but instead, for the first few weeks, the animals seemed tired and lethargic and slept for hours every day. Whatever the biophysical reason for it, a massive increase in the complexity of an environment seems to make a bear tired and increase the amount of sleep he needs. For that reason we allowed Bärle to sleep as much as she wanted to.

Bärle was slow-moving, methodical, and most often gentle in her approach to things. We watched her carefully and questioned any behavior that could indicate a problem. Six days after her arrival, when Bärle walked over and sat down to greet me, she seemed to favor her front left paw. I raised my right hand and placed it on the mesh above her left foot, since a bear will often place his opposite paw on the mesh against yours. I am not certain if they do this as a greeting, in play, or for some other reason, but it is a very handy behavior. If you need to see a bear's front paw pad, you can often entice the bear to show you his paw in this way. But Bärle broke eye contact with me and began to look around. High above her to the left, attached to the fencing, was a tiny shelf about one foot by eight inches, which was used as a platform to feed small primates. Bärle slowly got up, stood on her hind legs, and grabbed the shelf with her left paw in an odd attempt to hoist her huge bear body onto it. I was confused. Then it hit me. Bärle was trying to perform a circus trick for me, at my command! I felt sick, and instantly removed my hand to undo the voodoo I had begun. Bärle stopped, but the damage had been done. She paced on and off during the next twenty-four hours. After that I was careful not to raise my hand, and I spread the word to the rest of the staff. We put an immediate moratorium on training for Bärle.

Two weeks later, I walked onto ward four in the morning and found Bärle pacing in the debris of used enrichment, straw bedding, toys, and dumped water from her stock tank. I checked the log book, but there was no mention of anything out of the ordinary. I suspected that Bärle had psychologically outgrown her environment. What had seemed large, complex, and challenging three weeks ago was now small, simplistic, and confining. We gave her additional enrichment, extra food choices, dozens of toys, piles of clean bedding, and a choice of nest-building materials such as straw, wood wool, and hay. The next morning it was the same thing. I found her pacing in what looked like an enrichment battlefield. She had upended and thoroughly experienced everything. This was actually good news, because it meant that Bärle's recovery was progressing. But it also meant that we had to act fast to significantly increase the complexity of her environment. If we allowed Bärle to stay much longer in what was now a substandard environment for her, we might not be able to stop her entrenched pacing behavior.

We worked quickly. Bärle was scheduled for a veterinary checkup the following day, for which she was to be immobilized. We decided to move her directly to the Arctic Ring of Life, or the ARL, as we called it, while she was still anesthetized. On short notice, keepers at the ARL cleaned and disinfected the entire building for Bärle's arrival, brought in fresh straw for bedding, and ordered additional food provisions. The following morning all the plans were in place. Bärle was immobilized and given a physical exam. Blood and skin samples were taken for laboratory analyses. One of her incisors was found to be loose and was extracted. We wondered if a toothache could have accounted for some of her reluctance to eat. Before she woke, we lifted her into a crate and transported her to the ARL.

This new building was well planned for bear living. There were ten rooms in total that averaged 140 square feet each. The room along the south wall became known as stall one, the room next to it was stall two, and so on toward the north wall. The eighth room was the last stall in the row, and we named it the pool room because it contained a four-foot-deep freshwater pool. It was adjoined to the cubbing den and a private stall off the den. The stalls were joined along the west fenceline by a hall with access doors into each room. In turn, each stall was joined to the next with an access door in the middle of the shared walls so that we could give a bear more room if required. Our plan was to give Bärle access to the entire building and keep the other bears outside for a few days to give her time to get to know the building and to be able to view the other bears without having to interact with them if she didn't want to. We placed her in stall one to recover. Here she would have privacy, because the hall ended there with an access door and did not abut the room with a fenceline.

Bärle woke a little after one o'clock in the afternoon, and by two o'clock she was sitting up and sniffing the walls. Other bears had been here before her, and she was quite thorough in her olfactory investigations. By three o'clock, Bärle was standing up and moving around. Once we were certain that she was fully awake, we gave her polar bear chow, soft canned dog food, and water. She was very interested in the sparrows that were twittering and flying around the rafters. Several birds had found their way into the building, and to free them we would have to wait until the evening, when they would be lured from the dark building to the outside by the entry door floodlights. For now, a sparrow would drop to the ground, hop over and pick up a small piece of polar bear pellet, and fly off with it. Bärle watched them from a distance, fascinated, and periodically tried to approach one.

In between sparrow-hunting sessions, she spent a great deal of time licking her front paws, grooming the fur, paw pads, and spaces between the digits. This was the first time we had observed Bärle taking an interest in cleanliness. Traumatized animals frequently lose interest in grooming and personal hygiene, so this development too was cause for quiet celebration.

To give Bärle time to get her bearings in her new home unencumbered by the nosy neighbors, we locked the resident bears outside overnight. At forty degrees Fahrenheit, the ambient temperature was unusually warm for December and was easily accommodated by the bears' winter coats and robust fat reserves. Being shut out of the proceedings, however, did not prevent their intense curiosity or keep them from their fact-finding mission. At intervals the bears crowded the outside door jambs, sticking their noses into cracks as far as they could and sucking back the inside air for information. They sounded like steam engines as they exhaled into the metal hollows between the doorframe and the slide. Their dogged determination to find out what was behind doors number one and two suggested they knew Bärle had arrived.

The following morning we attempted to bring some of our resident bears inside so that we could clean at least one of the two outside enclosures. We housed the bears in two groups because the two unrelated male bears, Adak and Triton, did not get along. Triton, the younger male, was born in 1997 at the Roger Williams Park Zoo in Rhode Island. He was separated from his mother when he was two years old, the period of natural dispersion, and was moved to the Detroit Zoo. Since he was a subadult cub, attempts were made to integrate him with Adak, the older male. At first Adak tried to subdue the energetic and aggressive Triton in wrestling matches. When that failed to restore peace, Adak allowed him to win the contests for dominance. This also failed to bring peace, since Triton was relentless in his efforts to run Adak off. Running off another male works well in the wild because there the loser of the battle has somewhere else to go; in captivity, he does not. We managed that situation by creating two fluid groups in which the females could be with either male, depending on the bears' preferences and the breeding recommendations instituted by the AZA Bear Advisory Group.

We let Adak's group in because Adak was a smaller male. Triton was now five years old and weighed about nine hundred pounds. He wouldn't finish growing until he was about ten, and he

easily resembled the massive males who used to pick on Bärle and
Alaska in the circus. We decided not to bring Triton in until we had
observed how Bärle dealt with Adak across the mesh.

Adak's group included Sissy, Vilma, and Icee. Letting them in
was like opening the door to a classroom of excited schoolchil-
dren at recess. Four large, self-centered polar bears all tried to
cram their bodies through the doorway at the same time, pushing,
shoving, and woofing, scolding the other bears for being in the way.
Bärle was temporarily closed into stall one, where she could either
greet new bears at the mesh gate or move away from the door and
have her privacy if she wished. She chose to stay by the gate and
observe the bears.

Each bear dealt with the situation differently, according to
his or her personality. Adak walked up to the gate first to greet
the new female by licking Bärle's nose through the mesh, which
did not surprise me. Sissy also walked right up to the gate, stood
shoulder to shoulder with Adak, and licked Bärle's nose, which did
surprise me.

At twenty-six, Sissy was an old bear. She and her twin sister, Nikki, were born at the Pittsburgh Zoo in 1976 to a Canadian
polar bear named Snowflake, who had come from northern Quebec in 1968 as an orphaned yearling cub. How Snowflake came
to be orphaned is unknown. She lived at the Pittsburgh Zoo with
another Canadian male polar bear, named Snowball, who was also
orphaned in northern Quebec in 1968 under unknown circumstances. Snowball died in 1978 at age eleven. Snowflake, Nikki, and
Sissy lived together at the Pittsburgh Zoo until 1993, when Sissy
was separated and moved to the Columbus Zoo, where she lived
for five years.

In 1998, the Detroit Zoo brought the family together again in
preparation for the completion of the ARL. Sissy showed signs of
recognizing her mother and sister by favoring their company over

that of the other bears in the group. Sadly, Snowflake died in February 2001, just before the opening of the ARL. Sissy and Nikki moved over to the new facility with the other bears in the fall. Nikki had an outgoing personality and was quite interactive and opinionated with the other bears, and she had Sissy's back during bear squabbles. Nikki most often kept company with Jewel, who had arrived in 2000 from the Abilene Zoo, where she was born. Sissy was a reserved and self-determined bear who seemed almost disgusted by bear quarrels, often leaving scenes of disagreements while expelling huffy rebuttals. Her seemingly out-of-character greeting was possibly an indication of genuine interest, maybe even goodwill. I was scrutinizing the bears' responses to each other, looking for behavioral clues that would help us to develop an integration plan that would set the bears up for success.

Adak was a small, stocky, twenty-four-year-old male bear who had been castrated, and from a distance his silhouette resembled that of a female bear, depending on the angle. "Poor Adak" was a frequent refrain muttered by sympathetic but slightly amused zookeepers, and his behavior often met with the disapproval of intolerant females who woofed, jaw-snapped, or paw-slapped him in the head, ran away, or simply tolerated him. He could be raucously playful but also clumsy and lacking refinement in his breeding advances toward the females. He regularly dispensed with the traditional polar bear courtship behaviors and manners and simply mounted females willy-nilly. Walking right up to Bärle to greet her across the mesh was his typical *modus operandi*.

When Vilma entered the building, she moved aggressively toward Bärle but stopped short of coming face-to-face with her. She expressed a quick, pointy upper lip, indignantly made a slight, quick stomp with her front paws in Bärle's direction, and left. Knowing Vilma, I suspect that she could have been annoyed at any number of things that had less to do with Bärle's presence and more to do with her own comfort. Vilma was a twenty-year-old, robust, self-centered female bear who was born in 1982 at the Zoo Leipzig in Germany. At only eleven months old, before the period of natural dispersion, Vilma was separated from her mother and sent to the Kolmården Wildlife Park in Sweden. A year later, she was purchased by animal dealer Fred Zeehandelaar and in November 1984, at the age of two, was sold to the Detroit Zoo.

Vilma was smart but bossy. Ownership and control mattered to her, and those traits could lead to disputes. Her prickly disposition often caused her to be left alone, but she didn't seem to mind, preferring to spend hours playing with her blue ball in the pool.

Icee did not come inside with her group until several days later, and then she stood in the doorway for twenty minutes, watching Bärle and smelling the air. Her concern about the arrival of a new bear could have been mixed with concern about the change in daily routine. The other bears were locked outside day and night for a few days to accommodate Bärle's acclimation. Icee spent some time pacing outside to ease her discomfort.

Icee was a twenty-one-year-old bear, born at the Columbus Zoo in 1981. At one year old, she was separated prematurely from her mother and moved to the Detroit Zoo. Icee frequently negotiated peaceable relations with the other females by taking the unwanted advances of male bears off their hands. She often tolerated Adak's less than elegant behavior and had developed a mother-lover-friend relationship with Triton. A new female in the group might mean competition, and it definitely meant renegotiation.

When the other bears had been shifted outside again to enjoy clean and enriched enclosures, Bärle was given access to the entire building. She spent her time taking two- to three-hour naps and exploring. She slowly went from room to room, meticulously collecting information and experiences by smelling, pushing, and pulling on doors, mesh, and automatic waterers, and investigating enrichment items. She had several knee-high straw nests, which she fluffed daily by turning over the top layers. She had lunch bags and boxes, a stock tank with half-a-dozen live trout that she quietly watched and sometimes chased, heavy plastic balls, a spool, and the freshwater pool, which we eventually filled to its full four-foot depth.

Each morning, Bärle carefully walked down the steps into the pool and submerged her whole body, leisurely rolling over now and then and washing her face. To our knowledge she had never had the opportunity to use a pool unchallenged by other bears. She had come out of her anesthesia with some stiffness in her hindquarters; perhaps bathing in the pool also loosened her muscles. We were all guardedly optimistic; Bärle's pacing had been vanquished again.

Although she seemed to be back on the road to recovery, she had suffered one important setback: she had lost her appetite again. Each day we offered her a smorgasbord that any bear would be delighted to gobble up, including herring, mackerel, lake trout, whitefish, polar bear chow, apples, pears, grapes, greens, and carrots. She would only eat grapes and canned tuna, and even then we had to be sitting with her keeping her company. So I went back to Farmer Jack's and bought several rotisserie chickens, which now the other bear keepers and I fed to her by hand. With a little smile on her face, while we sat and kept her company, Bärle lay like a sphinx and used her teeth to strip the crispy skin off aromatic chicken parts held between her paws.

Slowly she began to eat a few other things on her own. Her appetite fluctuated from day to day. I could usually gauge what kind of appetite Bärle had on any given day by the items I found in her enclosures. Two untouched chicken wraps lying on the floor next to Bärle meant that Betsie Meister, one of the zookeepers, had desperately sacrificed her lunch for the cause.

80   As we worked on Bärle's diet, we also forged ahead to broaden her horizons. It was exceptionally warm for early December; the temperature hovered just above freezing, and the sun was shining on and off. Bärle was doing well acclimating to her new environment, and she would come when we asked her to. It was time to let her go outside.

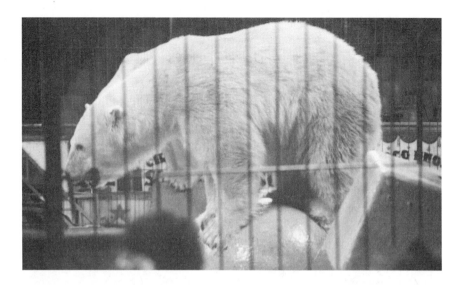

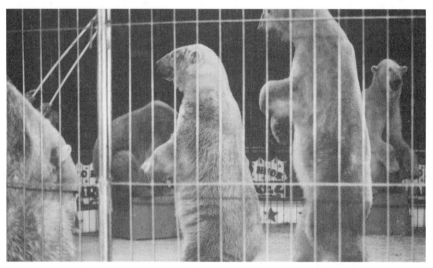

TOP In the Suarez Brothers Circus the polar bears suffered in the tropical heat while touring Mexico and other Caribbean countries, and performing before sweltering audiences. The bear in the foreground, standing on the ball, is thought to be Bärle. *Photo: Courtesy of the People for the Ethical Treatment of Animals (PETA).*

BOTTOM The tropical heat caused the bears to pant repeatedly during circus performances. Note the open mouths of all three bears whose faces are visible in the photo. The small bear in the foreground is thought to be either Bärle or Alaska. The other four bears are any of the massively huge males: Royal, Willie, Masha, Boris, and Kenny. *Photo: Courtesy of the People for the Ethical Treatment of Animals (PETA).*

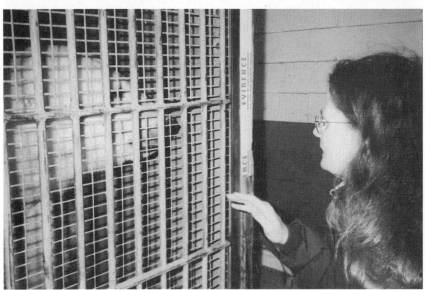

TOP Else Poulsen [center] quietly calls to Bärle in the shipping crate that she arrived in at the FedEx hangar in Detroit Metropolitan Wayne County Airport on November 19, 2002. A journalist [right] keeps his distance. *Photo: Courtesy of the Detroit Zoological Society.*

BOTTOM Bärle, smiling slightly, comes up to meet Poulsen, who raises her hand to touch the mesh end of the shipping crate in a greeting. Bärle's innocent, cub-like expression took Poulsen completely by surprise. *Photo: Courtesy of the Detroit Zoological Society.*

In the first week after their introduction on May 2, 2003, Bärle [right] repeatedly approached Sissy [left] to play. Sissy was not interested and grew increasing annoyed with Bärle's requests, which in turn annoyed Bärle. Note the pointy upper lips of annoyance displayed by both bears. Sissy emphasizes her displeasure by aggressively stepping forward and meeting Bärle head-on. *Photo: Courtesy of Tom Roy.*

Bärle discovered that the polar bears had visual access to the neighboring seals through large acrylic windows in the saltwater pool. Bärle spent countless hours stalking them, and never swayed from her conviction that seals were meant for hunting, hinting at her wild heritage. *Photo: Courtesy of Tom Roy.*

Bärle used several hunting techniques. One method involved hiding behind a pillar, waiting for a seal to swim by in the neighboring pool. These behaviors have never been recorded before in captivity because the Detroit Zoo is the only zoo in the world where seals and polar bears share a pool divided by acrylic windows. *Photo: Courtesy of Tom Roy.*

When a seal swam by, Bärle leaped out from behind the pillar and
sometimes crashed into the window in an attempted grab. Some of
the seals were visually impaired and seemed oblivious to Bärle's
behavior. The sighted seals had quickly learned that the polar bears
could not get at them, and they ignored Bärle. *Photo: Courtesy of
Carrie McIntyre.*

TOP Triton, the young, five-year-old male who sometimes weighed over a thousand pounds, bonded with Bärle. He otherwise enjoyed eating, napping, and playing. *Photo: Courtesy of Tom Roy.*

BOTTOM Triton plays ball in the freshwater pool. *Photo: Courtesy of Tom Roy.*

Male polar bears have been observed giving gifts to females during courtship and at other times. In the photo, Triton [left] has just given Bärle [right] the puzzle feeder between her paws. The gift was still loaded with treats. *Photo: Courtesy of Kathy Jo Ferguson.*

TOP Bärle [left] and Triton [right] spent hours playing together in the pools. Here, Triton is open-mouthed laughing, which polar bears do most often without expressing any vocalizations. *Photo: Courtesy of Tom Roy.*

BOTTOM Bärle [left] engages Triton [right] in a game of mouth-fencing. *Photo: Courtesy of Tom Roy.*

In early April 2005, Bärle brought her new cub, Talini, outside into the tundra enclosure for the first time. For the next few weeks, Talini stuck by her mother's side as if she were tethered. *Photo: Courtesy of Tom Roy.*

Talini explored and challenged herself in the natural enclosure under her mother's watchful eye. *Photo: Courtesy of Tom Roy.*

TOP Bärle entices Talini into the shallow freshwater pool in the tundra enclosure with balls and other toys. *Photo: Courtesy of Tom Roy.*

BOTTOM At almost ten months old, Talini entered her gawky stage with ears that stuck out in Yoda fashion, Bigfoot-sized paws, and the Roman nose of a bull terrier. *Photo: Courtesy of Else Poulsen.*

Bärle [below] gives a seal-hunting lesson to Talini [above], who dutifully hangs behind her, watching and learning. These behaviors have never been recorded before in captivity because the Detroit Zoo is the only zoo in the world where seals and polar bears share a pool divided by acrylic windows. *Photo: Courtesy of Carrie McIntyre.*

TOP Bärle [below] teaches Talini [above], floating above her, how to stalk a seal. *Photo: Courtesy of Carrie McIntyre.*

BOTTOM Talini practices her hunting skills on a gray jacket left behind in the underwater viewing tunnel of the pack ice saltwater pool. *Photo: Courtesy of Carrie McIntyre.*

Adak [background], who was repeatedly thwarted by the adult female bears at the Detroit Zoo for his oafish behavior and was often referred to as Poor Adak by bemused zookeepers, became such a caring and skillful guardian of the subadult Talini [foreground] that he earned a new nickname, Uncle Adak. *Photo: Courtesy of Carrie McIntyre.*

Winter after winter at the Detroit Zoo, Bärle never missed an opportunity to celebrate the arrival of a fresh snowfall by rubbing, rocking, and rolling her entire body in it in a gyrating dance of joy. *Photo: Courtesy of Betsie Meister.*

5

A POTHOLE IN THE ROAD TO RECOVERY

Bärle's Quarantine Revisited

IT WAS DECEMBER 18 and the kind of day that meteorologists remarked on as being the threshold of winter, anticipating a change in season. The air was fresh, and the temperature was slightly above freezing, with a warm wind blowing from the west. The sun was shining above clouds that were hazy gray with either rain or snow, but they were holding tight for now. The sky reminded me of many I'd seen in subarctic Manitoba and Ontario, the clouds filtering the sharp sunlight into soft, ashy hues. It was a perfect day to introduce a polar bear to the outdoor environment of our tundra enclosure.

The Arctic Ring of Life had two enclosures visually accessible to each other but separated by two moats and a boundary wall between them. Each enclosure was developed to represent a different ecoregion inhabited by polar bears. The pack ice enclosure on the south side of the moats was designed to resemble the islands of free-floating ice packed together to form a gigantic mat of ice in the Arctic Ocean from which polar bears hunt for seals. This one-acre enclosure featured a stream running into a 170,000-gallon saltwater pool visually shared with the neighboring harbor, harp, and gray seals and intermittently containing live trout and large blocks of ice. The tundra enclosure on the north side of the moats mimicked the treeless biome between the northern ice cap and the tree line, which was inhabited by oversummering polar bears waiting for the sea ice to form. This one-acre, natural habitat enclosure included soil for digging daybeds, grasses, topographic variations, a hillside cave, a thirty-thousand-gallon freshwater pool, and shady bedrock-like shores.

Much discussion had gone into the preparation for this day as we evaluated Bärle's readiness and considered contingency plans. We had worked out operation plans for as many potential problems as we could think of. For instance, what would we do if Bärle would not come back inside? What would we do if she panicked in the outdoor pool, which was gently sloped but became deeper in the center than the indoor pool? What would we do if she walked down the moat stairs but lost her way and could not find her way back up again? Our plan was to allow Bärle to make the decisions. If she chose to not go outside—no problem—we would wait and try again another day. If she chose to stay outside and not come in at the end of the day, we would give her indoor-outdoor access and monitor her throughout the night.

Assessing how much of a problem this would be likely also depended on which bear you asked. Since we only had two outdoor enclosures and we were managing three bear groups at the time, one group of bears would have to stay indoors for the day while Bärle explored the tundra enclosure. That group had to be Triton, Nikki, and Jewel, for one reason only: we didn't want to risk having Triton run up and down the pack ice side, calling over to Bärle on the tundra, possibly intimidating her, and making a giant nuisance of himself. So Adak, Sissy, Vilma, and Icee would be given access to the pack ice enclosure. They were older, less impulsive, and less hyper-energized than Triton. To make certain that the bears had things to do, we loaded both enclosures with lots of enrichment activities like lunch bags and boxes, puzzle feeders, scent trails, and additional breakfast and lunch foods scattered about.

At eleven o'clock in the morning, we were ready to give Bärle access. Earlier we had fed her breakfast in the pool room, which was adjacent to the tundra enclosure. The other keepers went outside to join our managers, who had gathered at the enclosure to watch what was for us a historic moment and for Bärle yet another challenge. Moving calmly, I opened the outside slide leading to the tundra. The noise of the hydraulic system attracted Bärle to the pool room's mesh gate, which we called "door nine," across from the open door. She sat down, and then I opened door nine. Bärle didn't move. I opened the gate into the back hall and sat down on the floor perpendicular to where Bärle was sitting with a mesh gate between us. We sat quietly. She breathed in the wind-borne scents for a moment, and then, as if having made a resolution, she crossed the hall and disappeared outside. I locked up the hall gates and went out to observe.

Bärle walked slowly on the grass, sometimes looking down at it, smelling it and the soil. Sometimes she repositioned a foot as if she had stepped on a pebble or twig that was uncomfortable or felt unusual. She sniffed everything in her path—rocks, sticks, enrichment items, vegetation, air, and her paws after stepping on things. She was not smiling; she was working, thinking. I wondered what memories, if any, this experience conjured up for her from far back in the recesses of her mind, memories from her first years on the true arctic tundra with her mother. Bärle reached the pool and tasted it, perhaps assessing its qualities. She circled the entire enclosure twice in her investigations. In a *grand finale,* she lay down in the grass, rolled over, feet in the air, and wiggled, wormed, and gyrated in a dance of joy that ended with her collapsing in an exhausted heap. Covered in grass, soil, leaves, and bits of debris, Bärle brought the outdoors in when she returned to the pool room. Her adventure had only lasted an hour and a half, but apparently it was over. I was relieved that it had gone well, a little surprised by its speedy conclusion, and somewhat amused.

Bärle was active on and off for the rest of the day in the building, interspersing enrichment investigation with napping. Her outdoor foray had primed her appetite, and she ate more than usual, consuming carrots, pears, romaine lettuce, and three pounds of herring, which we had to hand-feed her. As usual, Bärle did not eat any of the polar bear chow. I wasn't sure what the issue was, but if it was taste, I had to agree with her. Polar bear chow just tasted bad, at least to the human palate, slightly bitter and sort of mealy.

To give the other bears a chance to go outside again, we began work on the bear integration plan the following day. In a staff meeting, Sissy had been voted least likely to be aggressive with Bärle and most likely to develop a peaceable bond with her in an eventual introduction. Bärle and Sissy were given visual contact with each other across a mesh wall in the building.

Bärle was fascinated. She lay down and watched every move Sissy made. Sissy went about her foraging business, operating puzzle feeders and upending a lunch box. When Sissy was close to the fence, Bärle would move closer to the fence and watch. Adult bears will softly huff to get another bear's attention by quickly expulsing air through the mouth. I frequently use the word "huff" to get a bear's attention, and it works well.

Although Bärle purposely moved herself into Sissy's visual path, seemingly to get her attention, she did not call to her. Her body language reminded me of that of a small female spectacled bear I had worked with at the Calgary Zoo named Melanka. To get the attention of a male spectacled bear, named Nicholas, whom she was interested in during breeding season, Melanka climbed up to the top platform of her tree and waited until he was at the top of the tree in his enclosure, across the way. The distance was too great for her to call to him with a huff, so she began to jump up and down on her hind legs while holding onto a branch with her forepaws. Bärle could easily have used vocals to get Sissy's attention, since the distance between them was often less than ten feet, but she used body language only. There had to be a reason for this. Perhaps in the circus it had been unwise to get the attention of the big males, and Alaska had been deaf, so it was unlikely she would respond to verbal cues.

The following day, December 20, was a big day for both the zoo and Bärle. She was given access to the tundra enclosure again to help further her recovery. We would eventually introduce the other bears to Bärle one by one in the tundra enclosure, so it was imperative that she be comfortable in this habitat. The media had been invited to report on Bärle's progress to Detroiters. This was their first opportunity to meet her since her arrival, partly because she had been sequestered in quarantine but also because we were protecting her from the confusion and stress of having strangers around. Debbie Leahy from PETA had been invited to view Bärle for the first time since her rescue, and she flew in for the occasion. There was a controlled excitement in the air as journalists and camera operators vied for the best vantage points around the enclosure.

Triton was locked in again, and the other bears were given access to the pack ice. We set up feeding and enrichment opportunities in both enclosures and in the back for Triton. At eight o'clock in the morning, we were ready to give Bärle access. The other staff moved outside, and I opened the slide out to the tundra enclosure—which we called "door eight"—across from Bärle in the pool room.

Again, the noise of the hydraulic door opening brought her over to the pool room door. I opened it, too, with the intention of going over to sit with her in the hall to support her if need be. By the time I had shut down the hydraulic system, several minutes had passed, and Bärle had gone outside.

She walked slowly away from the building into the enclosure, picked up her front paws periodically, looked at and sniffed the pads, and then moved on. She stopped briefly at the top of the hill on the south side of the enclosure and saw Adak across the moat watching her every move with great interest. The females seemed to be more interested in feeding, and Vilma had spied her ball in the pool and was on her way down to play with it. Ignoring Adak, Bärle moved farther west, sniffing and mouthing small rocks, sticks, and vegetation. She circled around the west side of the pool, and coming back on the north side, she unceremoniously threw herself down and rolled and wiggled in the dirt and grass, upside down, legs everywhere, exuding a sense of abandon like a dog on the spring grass in the park. Then she collected herself and continued her journey. That's when I noticed she was carrying a foot-long twig in her mouth.

She investigated the cave and climbed to the top of the grassy hummock, lay down like a sphinx, facing west, and dropped the twig between her paws. The wind had picked up. She held her head high and with each breath allowed the scent-laden winds to fill her nares with microscopic particles and her brain with information. Her behavior was purposeful. She studied her new habitat for hours as the juices drained from her nostrils and mouth. Her glands were working hard. It was so dramatic that some of the spectators grew concerned and asked me if this was normal. All I could tell them was that I had observed this before in bears who had been moved from deprived to complex environments. It's as if their glands were waking up from years of olfactory deprivation.

We monitored the phenomenon; it reappeared the next few times that Bärle was outside, and then it disappeared.

By midafternoon Bärle had picked up her twig and gone indoors. Exhausted, she crashed in her straw nest with her stick beside her and fell asleep. It had been an extraordinary day. Debbie Leahy remembers,

> It was heartwarming... She looked so much better... Life in a circus is not for animals... any species... [the] constant confinement, life on the road, living in those cages, never stepping on a blade of grass! It reminded me that, even in my own life, we shouldn't take the simple joys for granted. I had invested a great deal of blood, sweat, and tears into this campaign but it was definitely worth it. Bärle, and others like her who are rescued from dismal conditions, serve to educate and inspire people. In Bärle's case, I imagine her story helped members of the public gain a greater understanding of the plight of animals in circuses, the plight of polar bears in the wild, and the plight of other bears still living in substandard environments."[1]

Bärle was still sleeping in the late afternoon as I was getting ready to leave for the day. That's when the bad news walked through the front door. Our associate curator, Michelle Seldon, told me that Bärle had tested positive for ringworm, which, contrary to its common name, does not always form a ring and is not a worm but a dermatophyte, a fungus that feeds on the protein keratin, the major component of the outer layer of skin. Although ringworm isn't fatal, it is highly contagious and is transferable from bear to bear by personal touch and exfoliated skin on the ground. Bärle had to be requarantined for forty-five days for treatment. Bärle's experiential recovery, which was moving along so well, had just come to a grinding halt. It felt like someone had knocked the wind out of me. The consequences of halting her journey into a more complex world could be grave and could catapult us back into a period of regression with a resurgence of frenetic pacing.

The staff and I shifted gears. An interim plan was made. Bärle was given access to the denning quarters that included the pool room, the cubbing den, and the adjoining private stall, as well as the hall that connected them. Fortunately, she seemed to like the apartment and had taken possession of it earlier in her recovery. She could not have physical access to the other bears, and so we would have to block the mesh door leading out to the main hall with several sheets of plywood. It felt as if we were putting her back into a box, but we had no choice. We would have to scrub and disinfect the entire building. And all of those places where Bärle had done the dance of joy, wiggling on her back in the grass on the tundra, now became contagion hot spots of ringworm spores. We had to make the tundra enclosure off limits to any bear until we had experienced several nights of freezing temperatures—fortunately, not a problem in December. And it was now up to us again to provide the substantial complexity that Bärle required to continue her recovery instead of relying on Mother Nature. With every step forward, Bärle's lust for complexity had grown exponentially. This was not going to be easy.

Bears are intelligent creatures. They are genetically endowed with the ability to negotiate a complex natural environment that requires them to be social with other bears, find seasonally ephemeral food resources every day, and navigate large tracts of difficult and dangerous terrain.

It is a myth that bears are solitary animals. They are, in fact, quite social. Female bears spend one to three years raising their young. Males and females are polygamous, courting and breeding with multiple partners, usually over a period of many months. During courtship, males corral females onto secluded breeding grounds where they share food and sleep together for days up to several weeks at a time. Occasionally, more than one generation of cubs may be living with a female. Bears can be tolerant of each other at large feeding sites such as salmon spawning grounds, large carcass feedings, berry patches, and garbage dumps. They position themselves within the feeding group by constantly making risk-management decisions based on familiarity with other bears and their stage of life.

Bears communicate with verbal and body language to illustrate intent and to ask for compliance. They utter specific sounds that have specific meanings, and will use that sound to communicate the same meaning the next time it's relevant, much the same as we do with words. Bears may utter more than one sound consecutively—like a sentence—to expand on their meaning. They naturally augment their verbal communication with physical demonstrations to further convey meaning. Unrelated bears will share food resources, but frequently ask for permission to do so from those already at the site. They also share olfactory and visual information with each other, using trees as signposts by rubbing, scratching, and biting on them; these trees are fervently checked by neighbors. They may not live close to each other as chimpanzees do, but they are social at a distance. The extent of the complexity of their social relationships is largely unexplored, but anecdotal literature and observations of captive bears suggest that their ability to collaborate socially is considerable.

Andrew Derocher, polar bear biologist, describes polar bear social cognition as different from ours: "If we do not see or hear another human, we assume we are alone. A polar bear is never really alone if it can smell another bear."[2] Being social at a distance also suggests that bears may have a different spatial cognition from that of other species that live in closer proximity to their cohorts.

For decades the intelligence of animals has been researched and judged by a litmus test of *scala naturae*, the hypothesis of man's unilateral evolutionary ascension to supreme intellectual being based on wishfully anthropomorphic criteria. Truth is, when this ladder of nature was originally proposed by Plato and Aristotle in about the fourth century BC and elaborated in medieval times, God, angels, demons, stars, moons, kings, princes, and nobles all occupied higher positions than the average man, and there was no mention of women. When the concept was made over to ascribe the evolutionary ascent of human intelligence, we conveniently dropped God, heavenly bodies, and the royal family. Sadly, researchers began dissecting bits of animal cognitive behavior out of context in easily malleable captive species living in deprived environments. This atomistic view provided precious little insight into the true mental capabilities of the animals and distanced researchers from the fact that their test subjects were sentient beings.

In 1960, paleoanthropologist Louis Leakey enabled Jane Goodall to study the behavior of wild chimpanzees in Gombe Stream National Park, Tanzania, in an effort to learn more about the evolution of humans, commonly thought to be from apes. What rocked the world was Jane Goodall's discovery that chimpanzees used blades of grass and twigs as tools, dipping them into ant mounds fishing for hangers-on to eat. To make matters worse, when there wasn't a fishing pole available, chimpanzees made one by stripping buds and knobs off a branch. This led to Leakey's famous postulate, "Now we must redefine tool, redefine Man, or accept chimpanzees as humans."

Since no one was in the mood to accept chimpanzees as humans, researchers scrambled like ants in a mound grabbing onto new definitions of tool use, self-awareness, compassion, empathy, sapience, intentionality, brain size, and other believed measures of intelligence and sentience.

Goodall's greatest contribution to science was her study of the behavior of chimpanzees within the context of chimpanzee life itself, thus opening a window to the world of their complexity, intellect, and sentience—their worthiness. The scientific intelligentsia wasn't quite ready for this, and thus continued to redefine the criteria for attaining a prominent position on the ladder.

In 2012, a group of 1,996 neuroscientists attending the Francis Crick Memorial Conference on Consciousness in Human and Nonhuman Animals at the University of Cambridge signed the Cambridge Declaration on Consciousness, proclaiming that "humans are not unique in possessing the neurological substrates that generate consciousness." The declaration recognized that a large, irrefutable body of research identifies self-aware, emotional, and intentional abilities in animals that generate such behaviors as problem solving, tool use, and language. Thus, the measure of an animal's intelligence on a scale of arbitrary human abilities has become obsolete. Although this may not come as a big surprise to those of us who obediently take the family dog for a walk when he brings us his leash, the notion does matter to researchers. It levels the scientific playing field, and the game—this incessant competition to establish intellectual prowess—is over. Perhaps now we should humbly change the seventeenth-century philosopher René Descartes' famous axiom "I think, therefore I am," which dictates that if you can think you are self-aware, to "We think, therefore we are."

A study designed to explore the spatial memory of bears was recently carried out on four American black bears—a nineteen-year-old-female, her two male cubs, and one female ten-year-old adult offspring living in a substandard roadside mom-and-pop animal menagerie in Alabama. In the field of comparative psychology, spatial memory is typically defined as that part of the memory involved in an animal's ability to navigate his way around his habitat. This unaccredited facility has been subject to dozens of USDA citations, warnings, and animal welfare complaints by responsible members of the public and by one conscientious research student. The most egregious of these complaints included a pack of wild dogs repeatedly killing off facility wildlife, a wolf allegedly dying of thirst, lack of drinking water or clean drinking water, failure to seek proper veterinary care, a rodent infestation in the food storage area, and improper storage of medications. The menagerie was also cited for failure to acquire the proper research registration.

These four adult bears were overcrowded in an enclosure that was less than 16 percent of an acre. Consider that North Carolina, a more progressive state, has developed minimum standards for captive American black bears and has legislated that one or two bears be held in one acre with an additional one-eighth acre for each additional bear. Thus, that law requires four bears to have a minimum of one and a quarter acres of natural habitat that is 50 percent wooded with trees, shrubs, and other perennial vegetation.

The study bears were reportedly fed a monotonous daily diet of less than half a pound of high-protein dog food and four pieces of fruit, typically apples and oranges, twice a day, at ten o'clock in the morning and at five o'clock in the afternoon. High-protein dog chow is an inappropriate food for American black bear adults, whose diet in the wild includes at least 85 percent vegetative matter. There was no mention of the bears being fed more in the fall and less in the winter to accommodate their natural biological changes in nutritional needs to accommodate hibernation. Wild black bears in Alabama hibernate, and so the warmer regional climate cannot be used as an excuse to not offer these captive bears seasonally appropriate nutrition.

Neither were these bears given variability in their daily diet or significant enrichment programming. In addition, food was used to lure the bears in and out of the building, suggesting that they were neglected by their caretakers, since bears will come when called by name to zookeepers they have a positive relationship with.

The researchers came to the banal and obvious conclusion that the bears used a feeding strategy similar to what they might use if they were eating at a berry patch, moving from bush to bush. Could it be any other way, because their enclosure, their entire world, is roughly the size of an average berry patch? The fundamental fact that these bears lived in a substandard environment and were neglected animals received only a brief mention. Any reference to the bears' mind-numbingly simplistic environment was opportunistically framed in a discussion of the need to do further research with bears in "substantially larger enclosures, under semi-naturalistic conditions, or even better, in the wild"[3] to assess a bear's abilities with spatial memory. In the wake of the Cambridge Declaration on Consciousness, this sort of junk science that allows the substandard care of bears under a shroud of scientific legitimacy is particularly offensive, rendering the researchers culpable for the bears' continued suffering.

In his work rehabilitating orphaned zoo bear cubs for eventual release into the wild, bear behavior expert Charlie Russell observed that bears are excellent navigators. In a personal communication he stated:

I have observed definite displays of very good spatial memory, even in very young cubs. I went for walks with my cubs almost every day, sometimes twice a day. These walks often covered many miles in all kinds of weather. I would start the cubs on these walks when they were quite young, just out of the zoo—like early May of their first year. Certain cubs would like to lead the walks, which I would let them do, but when we were in strange country they wanted me or my assistant to lead. I noticed that as soon as they had been led on a particular route these leader bears, usually a female, would always want to take over the lead. They would demonstrate perfect recall of the sometimes complicated route, even though they had only been on it one other time. Sometimes when they took over the second walk, it was very different from the first time when I was leading, which might have been deep in snow at that time. When they did it, it was bushy instead of a wide snow field. It was very impressive.[4]

In addition, Russell had observed that the leader cubs would sometimes veer off the trail into the bush at unfamiliar angles to take short cuts to their favorite spots, showing that they were able to navigate unknown terrain.

It is so widely accepted that bears have an extraordinary spatial memory and ability to navigate their environment that many provincial and state wildlife departments no longer consider translocating so-called problem bears an effective means of dealing with human-bear conflicts, since the bears tend to come back. Research indicates that 80 percent of adult American black bears return to their home range. Subadult males who are seeking to re-establish themselves away from their natal area tend to return only 30 percent of the time, while subadult females return 60 percent of the time. These staggering data for wild bears have led government departments to refocus policy and efforts on educating the public about their responsibility in eliminating bear attractants rather than on bear relocations.

Like chimpanzees and hundreds of other species, including ants, bears use tools. The literature is full of anecdotal descriptions and photographs of bears using tools to serve a purpose. A young male polar bear was photographed at the Tennoji Zoo in Osaka using a long wooden pool to knock meat out of a bucket hanging above his pit enclosure. The bear's second method of retrieving the food was to throw a small piece of plastic pipe at the bucket to topple it over and allow the meat to drop out.

In April 1972, bear biologist Henk Kiliaan observed the aftermath of a wild polar bear's possible tool use:

On April 10, 1972, while I was sledging with two Grise Fiord Eskimos across Sverdrup Inlet, Devon Island, to collect data on polar bear productivity, one of the guides remarked that a few miles back he had observed a place where a polar bear had smashed in the snow roof of a seal aglu with a piece of ice. The three of us returned immediately to investigate.

The aglu had been dug out to form a small crater. The snow roof was composed of very dense snow and was approximately 1 m [3 feet] thick. The breathing hole, which by now had frozen over, was about 0.5 m [1.5 feet] in diameter. The bear tracks were still very clear and were probably not more than 6 hours old. From the size of the tracks it was estimated that the bear weighed between 100 and 200 kg [220 and 440 pounds]. She was accompanied by two cubs. A bear of that weight would possibly have difficulty breaking through such a dense snow crust. Lying on the edge of the excavated aglu was a piece of fresh water ice about 80 cm [2.5 feet] long and weighing about 20 kg [44 pounds]. A drag trail which originated 6.5 m [21 feet] away led to the broken-open aglu. On examining the point of origin we discovered, partly concealed under the snow, a large piece of freshwater ice weighing several hundred kilograms frozen into the sea ice. We could see that the bear had smashed off the 20 kg [44 pounds] piece. The breakage surface, unlike the rest of the ice block and its surroundings, was free of snow. The bear had then rolled the piece of ice to where the aglu was located. By checking the tracks, we made certain that the adult and not the cubs had rolled this piece of ice."[5]

The researchers concluded that the bear could have broken off a piece of ice and used it to smash through the roof of the den or to try to smash the seal on the head or used it in play or to kick around in frustration after a failed hunting attempt.

Bear biologist Chuck Jonkel experienced a similar event suggesting polar bear tool use. To study the bears near Churchill, Manitoba, in the fall of 1971, he had set cable foot snares. When he arrived back at the site, he found tracks indicating that the bears had sprung the snares using small rocks from the site. He then removed all of the rocks from the reset snares. Upon his second return, he found that the bears had moved rocks as far as six and a half feet to spring the snares. This behavior has been recorded in other bear species as well. A male grizzly bear known as the Mud Lake Bear No. 146 in the South Fork Study in Montana was photographed at trap sites having set off leghold snares repeatedly using rocks, sticks, and tree branches.

The definition of tool use in comparative psychology is often narrow, highly subjective, and in my opinion, skewed toward humankind—again. If bears use their built-in tools, their ample claws, to scratch that itch or to comb out their fur, which they frequently do, it doesn't count as tool use because they did not use a stick or a stone. By definition, the tool has to be a separate entity from the body and an entity not attached to the ground, like a tree or a boulder. So if a bear uses a tree trunk to scratch his back because no small unattached implement works for an eight-hundred-pound itchy bear body, it isn't considered tool use either. Interestingly, bears typically go fishing for sticks and stones when they are sitting in shallow water.

I have frequently observed male and female captive-born and wild-born adult polar bears, as well as cubs at the Calgary and Detroit zoos, fish for pebbles and sticks from the bottom of the pool they were sitting in and holding the pebble or stick against their cheeks for a few seconds before dropping it. I cannot say that they were using it to comb or otherwise clean their fur. Any ideas that I had that this behavior was fur grooming using a tool were dead in the water when I watched the polar bears press dead fish against their muzzles.

Although rare on polar bears, sweat glands have been found on their jowls, some of which are active and some inactive, as well as on the soles of their front and hind paws. Perhaps placing cool stones or other items like cold, dead fish against the glands feels good. Or perhaps the behavior serves another purpose, like putting pressure on a gland to express it. As bear rehabilitator Ben Kilham commented in a personal communication, "Why didn't the bear scratch (his muzzle) with his claws?"[6] as opposed to using sticks, stones, or dead fish. Understanding bears is about asking logical questions. They are intelligent, sentient creatures, and their behavior is so complex that it confounds researchers and defies traditional definitions.

After Seldon and I collaborated with some of the keepers on plan B, I went back into the building and sat down on the floor at an angle, with my shoulder toward the mesh fence. Bärle came over to keep me company and sat with her shoulder toward me. We both stared into space, just hanging together. When a bear wants to communicate, she makes eye contact; when she just wants to keep company, she saunters up, sits at an angle, and looks at other things. For this moment, Bärle and I were just keeping company. It had been a wonderfully eventful day for her. How were we ever to keep this intelligent creature significantly occupied to further her recovery in the next forty-five days?

6

THE LANGUAGE OF BEARS

Bärle's Vicarious Learning

THE NEXT MORNING, the keepers were uncharacteristically subdued. Although none of us were at fault, we all felt guilty. The clock started ticking on Bärle's requarantine as soon as we could get the plywood boards up on door nine and begin combating the ringworm with an antifungal agent, but first we had to tend to the other bears. Our crestfallen spirits were trampled into irrelevancy the second we opened the pack ice slide. Adak, Vilma, Sissy, and Icee came thundering in like stampeding buffalo, pushing and bawling. They were hungry and more excited than usual. Then it struck me: with the appearance of a new female in the group, breeding season was coming early. I argued with that thought, as if I had a choice. We didn't have time for breeding behaviors right now, because they would throw every bear into a hyper-energized frenzy of emotions and personal agendas. As it was, Nikki wouldn't come all the way inside from the pack ice enclosure but·confounded both bears and humans by standing in the middle of the doorway. Jewel became a ghost bear, completely disappearing at times when called to come inside; it seemed she was tired of rambunctious Triton. And then there was Poor Adak, whom everyone wanted to thump at some point or another.

I put it all aside for later consideration and dealt with the day ahead of us. To keep Bärle from interacting with the bears in the hall through the mesh of door nine, we hand-fed her through the fence on the opposite side of the pool room. We kept her company for the two hours it took to feed the others, clean and scatter food and enrichment on the pack ice enclosure, and send some of the bears back outside again.

Bärle's appetite was good after her foray into the tundra enclosure the day before. She ate more readily when we quietly hand-fed her and kept her company. As boisterous bears argued over who got to eat in what room and with whom, and hydraulic doors closed behind those bears who had settled in, Bärle ignored it all and remained calm, absorbing the attention she was receiving at that moment. In my experience bears immediately recognize when things have improved, and they take full advantage of it. I guessed that life in the circus might have offered a few stolen moments here and there of positive attention and tasty treats.

Since the tundra was off limits to the bears for a few days while we waited for the weather to decontaminate it, we had to time-share the pack ice. One of the two males had to stay in the building with whatever harem of females wanted to be with him. Because of the AZA Bear Advisory Group breeding recommendations, Triton could only be with Nikki and Jewel, and eventually he could be with Bärle. Much to Adak's delight, Nikki, Jewel, and the other four females could be with him whenever they wanted to. This situation helped to increase the complexity and fluidity of their social lives and their ability to make choices. We carefully observed the bears' interpersonal behaviors each morning when they came inside to see who was traveling or keeping company with whom and who was avoiding or arguing with whom.

The bears understood the routine. When it was time to go back outside, they demonstrated their preferences by sidling up to the bears or door of their choice. Vilma, for instance, loved to play in the water with her blue ball and would try to stand near the door of the enclosure where her ball was. Sometimes we had to close off access to one outside door and funnel the bears into an enclosure where they needed to go. Today was such a day. We put all the females outside with Adak on the pack ice. Triton was given access to rooms one through seven with toys, treats, puzzle feeders, and a giant straw nest, but was kept away from the back hall and Bärle's apartment just down the hall.

When the building grew quiet, Bärle took a three- minute bath in her pool and then threw herself sideways onto the straw bedding and wiggled, rubbed, and gyrated, drying herself off. Then she collapsed into a two-hour nap. We didn't want to wake her, so we waited until she woke naturally to provide maid-service. We cleaned out all of the bedding in the den and the adjoining anteroom and scrubbed the floor and walls, knowing full well that we would only have to repeat this procedure as soon as the anti-fungal drugs arrived. Bärle lay like a sphinx and watched us work from across the hall, perhaps anticipating the fresh new bales of straw that we would leave her. Periodically she turned her attention to what we had initially thought was paw cleaning, licking her paws and snipping at them with her front teeth. The minute we finished and gave her access to the den and anteroom, she methodically went into her pool for a second, three-minute bath, completely submersing herself, rolling several times, and rubbing and washing her face. Then she wandered into the anteroom and threw herself onto the fresh, clean straw, rolling with her feet in the air, rubbing her back, rocking, and drying off. And then she fell asleep again.

What had surprised us was that Bärle had only gone to door nine several times throughout the day, sniffing, seemingly listening to the few times Triton made a noise, and trying to squeeze her right eye through the mesh to see down the hall. We had feared that she would spend all day at door nine waiting, listening, pawing at it to get our attention, asking to go back outside into the tundra enclosure. Bärle woke from her nap to the noise of our mechanical maintenance staff putting up plywood sheets to cover door nine. Our hearts sank as we watched her looking through the window of the anteroom to see that she was now being boxed in. We had a plan in place to provide for her now increasingly complex care. Before Bärle arrived at the ARL, our keepers had looked after all of the animals on the section throughout the day, including four bear species, three seal species, and arctic fox. Now we rotated the staff so that some keepers focused exclusively on the polar bears while others focused on the other bear species, seals, and arctic fox. This schedule gave us more time to spend on Bärle's special needs as she recovered and more time to prepare the rest of the polar bears for Bärle's integration.

Bärle's quest to go outside began in earnest the next day, when we found her waiting at door nine first thing in the morning. Bears are experts at detecting patterns of behavior or recurrences of phenomena in the wild, which is how they are able to arrive at salmon spawning grounds and berry patches at just the right time year after year. Their very survival depends on this ability. It was possible that Bärle had noticed that there had been an indoor day between her two outdoor days thus far. This meant that today would be an outdoor day. She occasionally broke her sentry duty at the door for a quick bath, some paw cleaning, and napping. She was unnervingly quiet and patient, sitting at the door, not making eye contact with us. Any one of our other bears would have huffed to get our attention, made eye contact, and then pawed vigorously at the door to get out. The less patient bears like Vilma, Triton, or Adak would escalate the request to a demand by huffing louder and more frequently, and paw-slam the door with the palm pad in annoyance if they were ignored. This behavior would be followed by short pacing jaunts, broken by sprints over to the keeper, locking in eye contact, hustling back to the metal door, and giving it a thunderous backhand, huffing throughout the entire demonstration. I wondered if it hadn't been safe to make requests of humans at the circus, or perhaps it was just futile.

Bärle's appetite waned. She ate some bread, a few herring, two mackerel, and a couple of carrots—not enough for an adult polar bear. The keepers brought out applesauce, butterscotch pudding, Cheerios, and raisins to try to prime her appetite, but she was not interested. In addition, she was still routinely leaving her polar bear chow. Over the next few days, we tried polar bear haute cuisine. We ground polar bear chow to dust in the food processor and used it to bake polar bear chow bread loaves. We served this with dollops of peanut butter, fish oil, fish blood, and salmon or pineapple cream cheese. Bärle alternated between licking the condiments off the bear bread and sucking off the tasty bits and spitting out the bread. Betsie Meister sacrificed her lunch yet again. This time it was granola bars that Bärle left after sniffing and tongue-checking them. Then Meister brought in a cooked chicken, and that seemed to change our luck. Bärle ate it, but only if we ripped the juicy meat off the little carcass and fed it to her in handfuls while keeping her company.

The cooked chicken idea was reinvigorated at just the right time. The antifungal medication Itraconazole had arrived, and now the countdown on her quarantine had finally begun. It was imperative that she receive her medicine each day without fail. We

doggedly pursued the cooked food idea and experimentally microwaved everything we could think of—yams, apples, and herring. We
learned that Bärle would eat cooked foods more readily than raw   103
foods and that microwaved herring smelled exceptionally bad in
our keeper kitchen, even to a polar bear.

Finally, we rediscovered canned tuna. Bärle would eat it with
some consistency, so we used this golden nugget as the delivery
mode of choice for her drugs. Perhaps cooked foods were easier
for Bärle to digest as her system changed to accommodate more
nutritious foods. Or perhaps Bärle had been given warm foods in
the tropics, whereas our foods often came right out of the coolers.

To bring some movement and life into Bärle's apartment, we
created a waterfall by climbing up onto the mesh ceiling of the
pool room and securing a hose with a nozzle that gently diffused
the spray over the pool. Then we seeded the pool with live rain-
bow trout. Finally, we dragged garbage can after garbage can of
fresh snow inside and dumped it onto the pool room floor, building a three- to four-foot mound. Bärle seemed to enjoy the snow.
She sniffed it, ate it, dug into it, rolled in it, and finally, like a cub,
fell asleep on top of it. She would sit under the waterfall in the
pool and watch the fish as they swam by, likely trying to avoid her.
Much to Vilma's annoyance, we temporarily absconded with her
blue ball and gave it to Bärle, who smelled it, tongue-checked it,
and then ignored it. Every day we gave her other novel items, like a
larger brown plastic spool, which Bärle briefly interacted with and
also ignored.

In the morning and throughout the day, she sat quietly by door
nine and listened, her ears moving in various directions following
the vocalizations and movements of the other bears. Occasionally
she would stick her nose through the mesh and breathe in deeply.
There was no doubt that she was picking up information about

the other bears. When the boards first went up, she still tried to cram her right eye through the mesh, testing whether she could somehow still spy the others. It was difficult for us to watch, since we knew that she had at least five more weeks of quarantine left. It was a tenuous time in her care. Having worked with trauma-tized bears before, I understood the delicate balancing act we were performing and the intense need for sensitivity to her psycho-logical state.

I returned from two days off over Christmas to find Bärle entrenched in pacing, taking three steps forward, three steps back-ward, and a half step at either end with a rhythmic head swing. The pattern was identical to what Debbie Leahy had observed Bärle do in her cage at the circus. For the first time since Bärle had arrived, she vigorously pawed at door nine to get out. The staff told me that they had tried to give her some sense of access to the outside by opening the building door at the end of the hall next to the mesh tunnel, an area we called the transfer. It crossed the hall connect-ing her pool room to the den and anteroom. But Bärle would just sit in the transfer, feverishly pawing at the mesh to just get out. She had gone from coping to snapping in just two days.

This was serious. What had changed? I went into my office and studied the daily logbook. There it was. A keeper who was not familiar with the delicate balance between recovery and regression had begun training sessions with Bärle. I reiterated our moratorium on training and put an immediate stop to the current sessions. But Bärle anxiously paced and pawed until that keeper was on her days off. The pacing ended and I breathed a sigh of relief.

Operant conditioning, which is used in accredited zoos today as a training tool and which is what the keeper was using, has its roots in B.F. Skinner's animal behavior research of the 1930s.

Skinner believed that for psychology to become truly scientific and thereby credible, one needed to be able to quantify behavior by measuring the stimuli applied to an animal and the resulting behaviors expressed by that animal. It is said that he considered the mind to be a black hole of subjectivity; therefore, his work focused on only the measurable. More is now known about the complexities of brain function, and as a result most psychologists today are cognitive psychologists rather than radical behaviorists, as Skinner was. Skinner's point about measuring behavior was well taken, however, and has helped to shape the field as a science.

Skinner used the term "operant conditioning" to describe how behavior can be shaped or changed by controlling the type of consequence experienced after that behavior has been expressed. He identified three types of consequences or responses. The first is a neutral response, which has no effect on the behavior. The second is a reinforcer, which increases the probability that the behavior will increase. Reinforcers can be positive or negative stimuli. The third consequence is a punisher, which reduces the probability that a behavior will be expressed again. We used positive reinforcement to train the bears by giving them food treats or verbal rewards when they expressed a desired behavior for husbandry or veterinary procedures. When a bear chose not to participate in a training session, there were no negative consequences.

In contrast, many animals in the entertainment industry are trained using aversive reinforcers or punishers, as Bärle was. A bear or other animal performs a trick to avoid being hit or otherwise hurt, bullied, or yelled at. If the animal chooses not to take part, the trainer frequently hurts the animal to reduce that behavior in the future.

On November 17, 2001, Debbie Leahy had witnessed such an incident while investigating the Suarez Brothers Circus:

106

The polar bears were not cooperating and Gafner seemed frustrated. When one bear refused to go down the slide, he climbed the steps and pushed her. Gafner looked angry that the polar bears were not responding to his verbal commands and nudging. As soon as the polar bears left the ring, Gafner with an irate expression on his face, exited the ring through the arena fence door (a temporary fence erected only for the polar bear act) and went back stage. He was gone for eighteen seconds. I could hear smashing and rattling that sounded like Gafner was beating bear(s) through the tunnel cage that is used for the polar bears to walk from their cage to the arena. When Gafner returned, he completed his act, which involved forcing the black bear to go down the slide backward and walk upright."[1]

Bears perceive, process, and learn from external and internal cues in their environment all day long. Jason Pratte, animal training coordinator at Omaha's Henry Doorly Zoo, is a twenty-year veteran in operant conditioning techniques at AZA-accredited zoos. In a personal communication, Pratte commented:

When we use operant conditioning (training) to shape an animal's behavior, we need to recognize that training is not just a tool to accomplish a specific goal. Training is teaching, and animals are constantly learning about us from how we behave. How we enter or exit a room, greet or not greet the bear, how we act around them in general... These are examples of when bears learn to act in certain ways around us, both now and later. The world around us is always learning something from our actions. Being aware of what we might unintentionally be teaching allows us to better understand the bears and the other animals we work with."[2]

Technically, the training sessions that the keeper had inno-
cently shared with Bärle had been successful, since she had
eventually participated by touching her nose to the target, a blue
and white buoy stuck to the end of a short doweling rod. This in
itself might seem harmless enough. But Bärle was not a lump of
clay to be molded by our institution's protocols. She was a complex, sentient being who had learned over the last seventeen years
of her life that training was frequently painful. The sudden recur-
rence of her frantic pacing and her escalated anxiety to get out of
the apartment were no coincidence. Considering her history, the
fact that Bärle took part in the training sessions did not necessarily
mean she was willingly participating. She likely made a risk-
management decision, concluding that participation might enable
her to avoid what she perceived as inevitable punishment from
humans for noncompliant behavior. How could Bärle understand
that bears were not punished here for not participating unless she
observed our behavior while training the other bears and came
to trust each of us personally? She couldn't. I reiterated that Bärle
would be included in training only if she chose to participate after
observing other bears being trained, and we would make those
opportunities available to her down the road.

Teaching bears to understand and comply with routine husbandry and veterinary procedures helps to create a positive,
low-stress environment for them. Pratte commented further:

> The positive reinforcement aspect of operant conditioning, pro-
> viding a reward after the desired behavior has been offered, has
> proven of tremendous value in managing animals in zoologi-
> cal institutions. By training with favored rewards, we can shape
> behaviors that not only allow better daily management, such
> as moving between enclosures or getting onto a scale, but we

can encourage them to participate in medical procedures that would be considered invasive or otherwise require anesthesia. For example, we can draw blood from a giant panda that has been trained to voluntarily place its foreleg into a special sleeve for a few pieces of apple, as opposed to having to fast the animal and dart it with sedatives to immobilize and collect blood. The first method provides the animal with choice and desirable consequences; the second is incredibly stressful and can result in injury, illness or in extreme cases, death. Training allows us to teach the animals what we want and reward them for participating, which in turn builds trust and reduces stress, thereby improving the animals' health and welfare.[3]

By New Year's Day, Bärle had settled into a new norm of decompressed living, without pacing. We frequently found her in the pool washing and playing when we arrived in the morning. She would dry herself off in the straw and then settle down in front of door nine to wait for the others to be let in. The sun, freezing temperatures, and snow showers had disinfected the tundra enclosure, and it was usable again. Turning her ears and taking deep nasal breaths, Bärle absorbed as much of the morning drama as she could when the other bears tumbled through the tundra slide across the hall from door nine. When the morning cleaning routine was over and the other bears had been given access to the outdoors again, Bärle often asked us to open the side door by sitting in the transfer and waiting or by pawing slightly at the mesh and making eye contact with us when we were nearby. This door led out to the service road that accessed the tundra via two sets of heavy metal service doors. When the wind blew in from the northwest, even I, without olfactory superpowers, could smell the bears on the tundra if I focused my attention on it. Each bear had a different smell, though they were all very similar. The scent of a clean bear is a combination of nutty and spicy. The scent of a dirty bear is neither nutty nor spicy!

Bärle busied herself with nest building, napping, upending puzzle feeders and other enrichment items, and paw cleaning. We were now beginning to suspect that Bärle's fastidious paw cleaning was related to irritation caused by the ringworm. On occasion she had rubbed small areas raw, causing slight bleeding. We added an antibiotic to her medications to offset the possibility of an infection. This required more personal feeding sessions to guarantee that she ingested the antibiotic. For us it was a joy to spend time talking to her, feeding her, and often just sitting with her quietly, keeping company bear-style. Her appetite increased again—a relief, since she had weighed in at only 458 pounds the week before. Bärle was beginning to show some muscle definition. When she had first arrived, she looked like a bear skeleton in a museum with a fur coat draped over it. Now she seemed to be slowly taking form, even if she wasn't gaining any weight yet. Bärle still napped several times a day, but she seemed more robust, sturdier, more alert, more bear-like. We were heading in the right direction.

Bärle's progress came at just the right time, since the needs of our other now hormonally charged bears were rampaging into our psyche and schedule. These normally rational, self-possessed bears were rapidly morphing into a single-issue interest group focused exclusively on sex—how to get it or how to avoid it. To fully appreciate the intensity with which bears respond to their genetic reproductive cues one has to delve into their behavioral norms in the wild.

Much about bear reproduction is similar across species; for instance, all female bears are thought to be induced ovulators, economically releasing their eggs only when there are courting males in the area. Equally frugal, impregnated females delay the implantation of the blastocyst until they have gained enough body weight to sustain themselves and the growth of an embryo. If the female does not reach a critical mass, she reabsorbs or ejects the incipient embryo. No one knows exactly what occurs.

The behavioral aspects of bear reproduction tend to differ depending on their environment. Most bear species live on land that generally does not shift in topography except for the occasional earthquake, flood, or volcano. As a result, terrestrial male bears defend a territory of a fixed size because they can be relatively certain that their food resources, largely plant life, will appear and reappear seasonally within its borders. Terrestrial female bears also live within a fixed territory, extending into numerous male territories. Thus, bears are polygamous. At breeding time, neighboring males and young rogue males seeking to establish themselves literally fight tooth and nail to court and breed with females.

Male polar bears are cone heads; their necks are wider than their head or jawbone, and satellite radio collars fall off. Females are similarly shaped, but their collars are kept on by their abutting ears. Therefore, much of the research identifying the movement of polar bears is based on data from collared female bears, bears tagged in capture-and-release studies, and expert extrapolation of ideas from existing biological principles. Male and female polar bears do not maintain territories but live in even larger home ranges, since seals, their food source, tend to move from season to season and year to year following fish, their food source, and the available sea ice. In this niche of nomadic resources, the intense battles between large males for breeding rights have over hundreds of generations genetically selected for enormous males who are twice the size of the females. Bear biologist Ian Stirling estimates that although the population is roughly configured of equal numbers of males and females, only one-third of adult females are available to breed annually because females rear each litter of cubs for more than two years. This further intensifies the rivalry for females, since there are three males to every female. In a testament to a lifetime of heavy competition, old, embattled males are frequently adorned with scars and sport broken canines.

Male polar bears kick off the breeding season by identifying where the females are and following them. In the wild, a male can follow a receptive female in an uncannily direct route over many miles, which leads researchers to speculate that females leave a biochemical signature in their tracks through either urine or specialized cells on their paws. This following behavior has led me to wonder about the true function of the sweat glands found on the bottom of the bears' feet. Since polar bears use behavioral means to adjust their body temperature, perhaps these glands are predominantly for scent marking. En route to and upon arrival at a receptive female, males may encounter other males following the same female and be challenged to a face-off.

From his personal observations, Ian Stirling comments on the courtship dance of polar bears:

> In the few times I have seen males challenged when with females, the female sometimes just stands and watches as if she couldn't care less. Other times, she will run away in the opposite direction, though maybe not so fast that the dominant male can't catch up to her. This is part of the courtship ritual, she runs away, he chases and circles around to one side of her to herd her back to where he is trying to keep her, or the direction in which he is trying to herd her if he is still trying to get her to a semi-isolated location where he can avoid other males to the maximum degree possible and interact with her for long enough until she is eventually ready to mate."[4]

The behavior of a breeding pair of polar bears can be anything from playfully rambunctious to serenely amenable to nonchalantly utilitarian, depending on the personalities involved and their history. With time or familiarity, the female will allow the following male to come progressively closer to her. Throughout courtship and breeding, males and females communicate intent to each other using vocal and body language. When the male is allowed within a shorter distance of the female, he often bridges the gap with a couple of giant leaps and meets her nose to nose. They talk in what sound like short, quick exhalations of breath, often accompanied by a chucking or clucking sound, which seems to come from the back of the throat.

Nose-to-nose soon becomes nose-to-cheek then neck-to-neck contact. The male may attempt to mock-bite the female, at which point she often punches him in the shoulder using an open paw pad and barks or roars at him to back him up. A smart male will back up slightly and stop neck-biting momentarily. He may instead try to instigate mouth-fencing, which generally seems to be much less offensive to the female. Both bears will fence with their mouths wide open, much as dogs do. Although a smart male makes a point of being less aggressive in response to female requests, a smart female does not thwart male advances too aggressively, as male polar bears can be dangerous. Courtship and breeding in polar bears can walk a fine line between mutual agreement and angry, growly outbursts.

As the male launches this frontal activity, he reveals his true intent by constantly attempting to circle around the female to her back side. In this reproductive tango, the female initially foils his rump-seeking behavior by skillfully realigning herself. Within a few hours to a few days, she is ready to breed and signals the male by rubbing herself against the male, the rocks, the ground, the pack ice, seemingly making contact with every object in the area. A female can also signal her intent by pumping her rump up and down in front of the male as if physically demonstrating the breeding activity.

Like wild females, captive females will mate with a second male in the same season if one is available to her. The preamble seems to be shorter in the second pairing, suggesting that the first male of the breeding season has to work harder at foreplay to bring the female into the correct biochemical mood.

There are numerous behaviors associated with breeding polar bears that may or may not occur, depending on the breeding couple. Some males may insistently bite the female in the neck to keep her stationary for copulation. This behavior seems to occur if the male is younger and less experienced, or if the female is reluctant or inexperienced and continues to move about. Gift-giving has been observed in captive male polar bears during and outside of the known courtship period. The male bear may bring her food, toys, or bedding materials. In both courtship and breeding, the female seems to have the distinct advantage; when she has had enough, she simply sits down and the game is instantly over. If there is tension between the bears, an experienced female will consider her behavior carefully so as not to anger the male. Males have been heard to call to the females as they approach, with a long, deep resonating bellow that sounds like an old lighthouse diaphone fog horn. Depending on a myriad of environmental factors and likely personal choice, a breeding couple can stay together for a number of days to a number of weeks, at which time each may move on to other mates or not.

The language of bears is similar among bear species, with some interspecies differences and some cultural differences between same-species groups. The gross similarity is that sounds are accompanied by simple or sometimes elaborate behavioral demonstrations with the intent to further the meaning conveyed. One of the most emphatic and easily discernible displays of communication between breeding bears is now a matter of public record in Bern, Switzerland. In 2011, managers of the BärenPark made plans to put their five-year-old male European brown bear named Finn back together with their ten-year-old female named Björk, who was raising her two female cubs, Ursina and Berna. The cubs were born at the BärenPark in December 2009, were sired by Finn, and would reach the age of natural dispersion, when they would normally leave their mother, in the spring of 2012. I was asked to work with the management team to plan the introduction, train staff, and assist in its execution.

Because the bears often do not have a choice in the matter, the introduction of additional animals into their habitat is one of the most stressful events in the lives of captive bears. There are only two motivators for survival in mammals—food and reproduction. Food is the primary motivator, and reproduction is the secondary motivator, which means that bears care about food all of the time and reproduction some of time. To introduce these four animals successfully into one peaceful, copacetic group, we used behavior-based husbandry techniques that take the bears' genetic and personal expectations into consideration.

Finn's genetic urges were relatively straightforward. Being a young male, come breeding season he would be interested in mating with as many females as were willing. Before, during, and after breeding season, he would be interested in food, play wrestling, food, napping, and food. Björk's agenda was more complicated and more mature. Genetically, she would feel the need to continue to raise Ursina and Berna and to protect them from Finn. When the cubs became subadults at two and a half years old, she would wean them and drive them off as her desires changed to breeding again.

The introductions would take place in two phases during breeding season. Several months in advance, Finn would be vasectomized to ensure normal male and female behaviors that we could work with. The objective of the introduction was not to generate young but to set up a social structure that worked for every bear. Finn and Björk would be introduced, and after they had concluded their breeding relationship, we would introduce the subadults, who had by now learned about sex by watching the adults.

The BärenPark enclosure is a large natural habitat exhibit that provides two acres of living space for the bears on the steep eastern shore of the historic River Aare, part of which has been diverted into the enclosure to form a naturally fed pool that runs the length of the exhibit itself. The enclosure can be divided into two separate living spaces when needed, both of which are connected to a building with numerous bear bedrooms. It is also connected to the historic bear pit, built in 1857, which is now only used as an enriched play area when the bears are waiting for the keepers servicing their large enclosure. Björk lived with her cubs in the larger half of the enclosure, on the south side. Finn lived by himself on the north side. This isolation was hard on him, because he was young and wanted to interact socially with other bears. Frequently, he would stand or sit at the dividing fenceline watching the cubs play and talking to them by huffing, clucking, and occasionally whining. When the cubs were younger, Björk would run up to Finn and tell him off in short huffy, lip-smacking tones. As the cubs grew older, Björk became less concerned and let them socialize.

In the spring of 2012, tension broke out between Björk and her subadult daughters. When Ursina or Berna tried to suckle off Björk's teats, she simply rolled over, moved an arm or leg, or just got up and left. The message was clear, and the subadults regressed into whiny, clingy, ill-tempered cubs. They would beat up on each other, as well as on logs, rocks, and toys, and sometimes even barked at their mother. All of their antics were to no avail; Björk was weaning her ill-mannered offspring whether they liked it or not.

To make matters worse for them, Björk now spent more time at the fenceline visiting with the attentive Finn. When Ursina and Berna tried to socialize with him, Björk chased them away with huffy, jaw-snapping remarks. Routinely, we had been setting up their feeding sites away from the fenceline to avoid aggressive behavior between Finn and Björk when the girls were cubs. Now, in preparation for the upcoming introduction between Finn and Björk, we scattered foods along the fence to promote cooperative feeding between the two adults and scattered additional foods in other areas of the enclosure for the subadults.

The intensity of discord between Björk and her daughters grew with time, and we realized that this might no longer be just about weaning. When Björk was sleeping or was otherwise occupied in the far end of the enclosure, Ursina would steal up to the fenceline and quietly huff for Finn to come over. If he heard her, which he didn't always because Ursina was so quiet, he would respond immediately. She would rub herself on the fence or roll on the ground, soliciting courtship behavior from Finn, who licked her face and smelled her body and rump whenever he could. Berna loyally followed Ursina wherever she went but kept her distance from the two of them and seemed utterly confused by the attention that only Ursina received. Despite the white noise of the flowing River Aare, Björk would invariably hear Ursina and Finn and charge Ursina at full throttle from across the enclosure, chasing her and Berna as far away as possible. Björk would then return to the fence to allow Finn to lick her face and smell her as she rubbed against the fence and rolled on the ground. Ursina was cycling and competing with her mother. Any questions we may have had about the true nature of Björk's aggression were answered when we observed Ursina urinating small puddles at the fence, just as her mother did. Finn dutifully came over to inhale these olfactory calling cards. Although Berna was not part of the dispute between Ursina and Bjork, she accompanied Ursina on her forays, watched Ursina's every move, smelled the urine puddles, and ran with Ursina as if she too were being chased.

Finn and Björk were introduced to each other on the morning of June 4 after they had both been given a large breakfast. We had drastically increased all of the bears' food resources for several weeks so that there was an excessive amount, communicating to the bears that there was enough food to sustain additional bears in the enclosure. Abundance of food is the key to ensuring peaceable integrations, since food is the bears' number one concern. The subadults were temporarily housed in the hyper-enriched bear pit for the day to give Finn and Björk lots of room to perform their courtship behaviors.

Finn immediately began herding Björk onto a suitable breeding ground. Being an experienced female, Björk was willing to be herded, but she directed the herding into the north side of the enclosure, where we ultimately wanted to house the subadults. Having previously observed captive brown bear males choose the feeding grounds as their preferred breeding ground, we quickly rained several buckets of favorite fruits and vegetables into the southeast corner of the enclosure, where we hoped the bears would go.

It worked. Björk allowed Finn to herd her to the southeast corner, where the two immediately began to mouth-fence and neck. By late afternoon Finn was biting Björk on the neck to hold her still, and they bred repeatedly. Orchestrating Finn and Björk's breeding ground so that it seemed to be their choice was vital. If it had not been their choice, we would run the risk of having them both nervously pace up and down the fenceline to go into the north side instead of focusing on breeding and relationship building.

We were now able to close the slides between the two sides of the enclosure and bring Ursina and Berna back into the north side. In one morning their lives had changed forever. Not only were they separated from their mother for the first time in their lives, but Björk was busy cavorting with Finn, whom she had always told the subadults to stay away from. The cubs were each stressed, possibly for different reasons, and they chuffed at each other and at their parents. They ran, walked, bolted from spot to spot, and smelled the ground, the rocks, the logs, the fenceline—everything. As far as we could tell, Berna was not yet sexually mature, since she was not expressing any recognizable signs of breeding behavior. She was going through the stress that every subadult cub goes through when being ejected from her mother's company and watching from a distance as her mother cavorts with what was supposed to be a dangerous male.

Ursina may or may not have felt separation anxiety; we have no way of knowing since her behaviors seemed breeding related. Her mother, whom she had been competing with for sexual rights, now had exclusive access to the male whom she had been trying to entice, and both of them were now ignoring her. Ursina and Berna stood at the fenceline, side by side, utterly rejected, watching and learning.

Over the next six weeks, Finn and Björk remained sexually active, although respites between copulation grew longer until whole days went by between breeding attempts. It seemed that Björk was less interested in breeding but was still competing with Ursina, whose interest in Finn had not waned.

One afternoon, Ursina was pawing sideways at the slide between the two sides, trying to push it open. Björk charged the slide from the other side, uttering a quick growl at Ursina, who immediately backed away. Finn, who had flanked Björk, moved up to the fence and quietly huffed, calling Ursina back. He then put his head on Björk's back as if to calm her or to include her. Ursina moved forward, and Björk growled and bluff-charged the slide again. Finn lumbered down the hill along the fence and huffed to Ursina, who responded by meeting him there. Björk flew over rocks and down the hill; charged the fence at Ursina, who backed away; and mock-bit Finn in the neck. She walked south, away from the fence, turning to wait for Finn, beckoning him to follow her. He did.

Björk stopped again and allowed him to mount her back. As Finn tried to breed with her, she resumed walking toward their chosen breeding ground with Finn awkwardly walking behind her bipedally, as if pushing a wheelbarrow. Björk's intentions seemed clear, and her message wasn't lost on Ursina, who had climbed up onto a hefty tree branch to watch, periodically stomp-jumping with her front paws and huffing softly. Berna safely watched the entire performance from her favorite nest high on the hillside.

By mid-August, Björk had lost much of her breeding steam, and although she did not approve of Finn and Ursina's meeting at the fence, she bluff-charged less often. Incredibly, she was still in breeding mode, calling to Finn, urinating in his presence, sleeping by the fenceline, and rubbing herself on everything in sight. Berna dutifully followed Ursina and was periodically able to interest her in play wrestling. Berna showed no signs of breeding behaviors herself.

On the morning of August 22, Finn and Björk were introduced to Ursina and Berna after they all had eaten a large breakfast in the building and we had super-enriched the large enclosure. We let the bears out, Finn and Björk on the south side and Ursina and Berna on the north side, as was the normal routine. When the bears were situated on opposite sides of the enclosure and engrossed in their enrichment, the keepers, who had been teaching the bears for months to understand the meaning of the words "opening door," called to the bears and let them know that the slides were opening.

Ursina caught on immediately and entered the south side through the lower slide by the river. Finn, who was also down by the river, saw her and ran toward her, huffing and clucking. Björk heard the commotion and stormed down to the river at breakneck speed. The chase was on. Berna joined her sister in being chased by their angry mother and an interceding suitor. The four bears ran the entire distance of the two acres several times before Björk had to slow down, feeling her middle age.

This gave Finn and Ursina time for courtship. They woofed, lip-smacked, huffed, clucked, licked faces, necked, and sniffed cheeks while dancing around each other. We had anticipated that at first Björk would be unhappy that the subadults were competing for Finn, but we also thought that because of their mother-daughter relationship, Björk would only want to exert dominance over the group and then settle into a new norm.

What we hadn't anticipated was Finn's remarkable ability to broker a peaceable living arrangement with Björk that included her two daughters. I have observed male bears act as peacemakers by placing themselves between two fighting females, but Finn's determination and ability to communicate his wishes were obvious even to visitors who happened by. Whenever Björk growled at Ursina and chased her and Berna around the enclosure, Finn ran between the females and met Björk head on. Quietly huffing and clucking and lip-checking her face and neck, he calmed her down. In a particularly heated scrap that sent the subadults racing away,

Finn hurriedly ran over to Björk, lip-checked her face, huffed quietly, and flanked and mounted her quickly. After that he came around to her face again, made eye contact, spoke to her in huffs, and then ran off to court Ursina. Staff and spectators instantly understood that Finn was communicating his interest in Björk even though he was also interested in breeding the other females. As a result, Björk stopped chasing Ursina and Berna for a while.

In that time, Finn also attempted to court Ursina, who was interested but moving around. He tried to position her by biting her neck to hold her still, but she kept turning around to see why he was biting her, foiling the breeding attempt. By midafternoon, Finn was being less assertive. A little confused by this change in tactic, Ursina pursued Finn and, remarkably, communicated her wish to breed by pumping her hindquarters up and down, effectively demonstrating the breeding motion. The message was clear not only to Finn but also to an astounded human public and to journalists, who later wrote about it. Today's teenagers did not invent twerking—bears do it to communicate their need to breed.

Finn tried again, and after several attempts, the pair worked out the details and bred repeatedly. Traveling as a breeding pair, the couple moved over to the wooded area of the enclosure and bedded down for a nap in a pre-existing daybed. Berna had been doing her best both to stay out of the way of angry, stampeding bears and to include herself in the breeding festivities, but to no avail. Her mother had ousted her, and now her sister was ignoring her. She was completely alone. Although Finn and Ursina were not actively chasing Berna off, they were simply too caught up in each other to pay attention to her.

Finn and Ursina resumed breeding behavior after their rest. Berna was poking her nose in personal places where it clearly didn't belong as she tried to ingratiate herself into the activities.

Nothing worked, until finally Berna hit on the key that unlocked the doors to the club. She positioned herself in front of Finn just as her sister had done and pumped her rear end up and down. This caught both Finn's and Ursina's attention. Berna had shown no other breeding behaviors indicating that she might be cycling, though I had speculated that Berna might become sexually mature within a few days to weeks under the circumstances. I was not convinced that she was cycling but thought that she was merely mimicking behaviors that might help to include her socially.

Surprised as I was by this young bear's ingenuity, I think Berna might have been more surprised by the outcome of her behavior. She didn't seem prepared to handle Finn as he attempted to mouth-fence with her and mock-bite her neck. She jumped away and then back again, seemingly unsure of what her response should be. The little grin on her face led me to believe she was not altogether alarmed by the game but perhaps misunderstood the purpose of Finn's preamble. Ursina, however, was not pleased, and attempted to chase Berna away. Again Berna seemed to misunderstand, letting Ursina catch her and instigating a cub-like play-wrestling session. Ursina acquiesced to the game and never chased Berna off again.

The following morning, Berna was taking part in mouth-fencing, necking, huffing, clucking, and breeding as if she were a breeding adult female. But the traditional signs of a female in heat were still missing. She was not rubbing herself against objects, rolling in the soil, or instigating following behavior in Finn. I have observed other adult females who exhibit no signs of courtship or breeding behavior but will allow aggressive males to breed them, possibly to secure their safety or to gain access to food resources. In this case it seemed that Berna did not wish to be alone. Wild subadults who have been ousted from their mother's protection frequently stay in small social groups. And now the Berna, Ursina, and Finn trio traveled, nested, and ate together. Finn alternatively bred with either subadult, as the occasion arose. Periodically, Finn broke from the group to spend time with Björk, giving Ursina and Berna time for rough-and-tumble play wrestling.

Like young Berna, Bärle was learning about bear behavior to secure a place in this local group of polar bears. But being cloistered away in quarantine without visual contact, she was at a distinct disadvantage. Each morning, she listened intently at door nine, squished her nose into any opening, and when bears passed by her door to leave or enter the building, sucked back the air to obtain information about them. Depending on the day's issues and events, each bear reciprocated by sniffing, huffing, or backhanding door nine from the other side. Apparently Nikki had had enough of this clandestine living arrangement, and in passing ripped off a small piece of the plywood in the upper corner of the door. Bärle immediately flattened her face against the board, jamming her eyeball through the hole for a look. It broke our hearts, but we had to replace the board as soon as we could get Nikki out of the hall—easier said than done.

Nikki, like the rest of the other bears, was in breeding mode. The concept of breeding season is fairly simple: male finds and courts female, who either wants to breed or not. But during this time, bears turn into mere hulls of their former selves and focus almost exclusively on satisfying their genetic urge to either breed or avoid breeding, depending on hormones or personal preferences. We had two males and five females. The number of combinations and permutations of bear couplings possible determined by daily mood swings was almost astronomical. This was turning into the most hormonally fueled, difficult breeding season I had ever worked with. Given the circumstances, I was not sorry that

Bärle's second quarantine had pushed back the introductions. It was simply too much to ask of the bears to both deal with their heightened sexual tensions and be cordial enough to make a good first impression.

In general, Triton seemed dissatisfied with how this season was going. Either he was with Nikki and Jewel, who would not tolerate his breeding antics, or he was alone, calling to females or·challenging Adak from across the moat. In all scenarios he was ignored. When Nikki and Jewel were not cycling, the two friends allowed Triton to sleep with them in the cave under the hummock on the tundra. When one was cycling, she would attract Triton's attention, sending the noncycling female heading in the opposite direction since she would not want to be around a courting couple.

Nikki would not come inside the building for days at a time, likely because the rooms were not large enough to avoid a breeding male or to allow for courtship behavior. She would stand or lie down in the doorway so that we couldn't close the slide. This was a handy technique for her to observe the activities and assess what was for breakfast, and yet still not be locked inside. As a result, we could not clean the outdoor enclosure. On occasion she would dine and dash by running into a bedroom, grabbing several mouthfuls of breakfast, and racing back outside. To reassure her, we changed our routine and stopped locking her in when she did decide to come in to eat.

Jewel would come inside—sometimes. She seemed to move in and out of breeding mode several times over the weeks. When she was in breeding mode, she would display pelvic thrusts to males and females alike; rub herself against fencing, enrichment items, the floor, and almost everything in the outside enclosures; and frequently growl at Triton when he showed an interest in her.

Both Jewel and Nikki had developed small, raw hot spots on their skin. These spots would heal, but then others would erupt someplace else. The veterinarians had determined they were not related to ringworm. On one occasion, a less experienced veterinarian suggested that we make the bears eat more bear chow since its formulation ensured a proper nutritional balance. With the exception of Bärle, the bears had all lost dozens of pounds since breeding polar bears frequently lose interest in eating. Triton alone lost close to two hundred pounds in just over two months. It was next to impossible to get him to concentrate on eating much of anything. His entire focus was on competing with males, courting females, and breeding. We made a valiant effort and created Italian seasoning–flavored bear chow bread, which was a flop. However, Nikki and Jewel loved to lick fish oil off the loaf and cast the bread aside. We felt lucky to get vitamin E into them by mixing it with canned dog or cat food. The keepers and I became expert antiseptic spray shooters at the hot spots as Nikki and Jewel darted in and out of the building. We were to learn months later that these hot spots were just the tip of the iceberg and indicated more than just a skin disorder.

Sissy and Icee showed more stability in their breeding behavior. Sissy stayed in breeding mode for weeks. We had the veterinarian check her when we noticed that she was bleeding from her vaginal area. I have observed this phenomenon in other female bears, but it seems to occur infrequently. Triton confirmed the doctor's diagnosis that she was cycling by sitting in front of her bedroom for half an hour. A few weeks later, when she bled again, Triton charged the door four times to get to her. When that failed, he wandered the hall moaning, huffing, and woofing. We were finally able to move him onto the pack ice enclosure, where he continued his wandering up and down the moat, calling to the girls on the tundra. They ignored him. Icee had taken to Triton, since he was a subadult cub. Unlike the other females, she tolerated his incessant mounting behavior as he learned about breeding behavior.

When Icee cycled it was only for several weeks, but much to Triton's delight, Icee welcomed his advances and presented her hindquarters to him, despite the fact that there was a mesh fence between them.

Adak had also been roaming from female to female, trying to ascertain their willingness to breed, but his attempts were met with either resistance or short-term tolerance. He hit pay dirt when Vilma cycled. She immediately coupled with Adak, and they stayed together as a breeding pair for weeks, despite Triton's bellowing protests from across the moat. Adak and Vilma made an interesting couple. They were both blunt in their dealings with other bears, but they got along well during breeding season, traveling, sleeping, and eating together.

Bärle listened intently to this soap opera of sometimes entropic and sometimes cataclysmic bear events, learning about each bear. I too was waiting, learning, wondering whether Bärle was going to cycle or whether she was in fact cycling but not displaying any breeding behaviors. We had no indication of any hormonal changes, but we noticed that she was settling in. She had set up her own daily routine, taking her breakfast over to door nine to listen to the other bears. She bathed in the morning, took long midday naps, and worked on her nest. A few food items, such as whole feeder rabbits, were so prized that she brought them into her nest in the maternity den for safekeeping. She also absconded with a whole leg of lamb, which she buried deep in her straw nest. She sought out our company, and we all began to notice a new behavior. When we sat with her just to visit, she made eye contact with us and opened her mouth. At first we thought she might have a dental problem, but then we realized that she was asking us for food. We were ecstatic; Bärle was communicating with us! The onus was now on us to respond whenever she asked in order to keep the relationship moving forward.

On January 28, we immobilized Bärle so that we could take three biopsies to see if the antifungal medication was helping her. Ann Duncan estimated that 80 percent of the fungus had dissipated but that she still needed another round of drugs for three more weeks. Ordinarily, I would have been disappointed, but considering the sexual rodeo that was taking place on the other side of door nine, I was not unhappy. We had at least three more weeks for Bärle to gain strength and develop a trusting relationship with us and for the hormonal storm next door to pass. Bärle was released from quarantine on February 26. It was time to begin the introductions.

7

A GOOD FIRST IMPRESSION

Introducing Bärle

So, HOW DO you communicate to a bear that there will be enough food for her and another bear? You do it the bear way: by demonstration. Bears do not think of food in terms of breakfast, lunch, and dinner, like humans do, but in terms of resources.

I have spent countless hours observing wild bears in social feeding situations at berry patches in Montana, Alberta, and northern Ontario. Bears situate themselves at an unobtrusive spot and begin to eat. As they eat, they often lift their heads to scan the entire berry patch, seeming to assess how much food is available and how many bears there are to share it. In any given situation, a bear wants to know whether there is enough food for all the bears.

A week or two before we introduced Bärle to the other bears, we had to significantly increase the amount of food available to let them know that there would be enough food for all. In the first few days of increased food, the bears will eat themselves silly, much to the horror of the average zoo dietitian. As the days go by and the bears begin to trust that the increase in resources is here to stay, they go back to a seasonally appropriate food intake, leaving the excess.

When hormones wane at the end of breeding season, both wild and captive bears seem to relax and maintain their interest in socializing with other bears. As a rule, this is the best time to introduce nonbreeding captive adult bears. Although we hoped that Bärle might eventually be interested in breeding with Triton, that was down the road. He was at least twice her size, and it was no coincidence that Bärle consistently moved away from the door the few times we had allowed him to pass by. She had spent years dealing with very large, rightfully angry, aggressive male bears who were stressed beyond the breaking point. Our immediate and very serious concern was to set up the introductions so that Bärle had choices, was safe, and could replace any poor decisions she made with better ones as she learned.

Throughout the introduction process we would rely heavily on environmental enrichment. Enrichment events, such as scatter feeds, puzzle feeders, bedding material, and branches to nest build with, help to take attention away from the fact that there is a new bear in the mix. They offer the bears an activity to nonchalantly feign interest in while deciding on the best course of action. This displacement behavior serves a vital role in decompressing a situation. A bear can appear to be nonaggressive and even indifferent while thinking through the options. I have watched bears pretend to investigate insignificant things like a single raisin on the ground while covertly taking quick side-glances at a new bear.

One of the common mistakes frequently made in captive bear introductions is to try to fit the newcomer into the pre-existing bear group. This tactic only strengthens the current social structure, warts and all, and further disadvantages the outsider. In this situation the new bear is frequently scapegoated and bullied. We planned to systematically take apart the old group and build a new group around Bärle, giving her a chance to establish herself with each bear on a more equal footing. Our resident bears would be somewhat destabilized, but rather than defaulting to old behavior patterns, they would have to think their way through new social interactions and be on their best bear behavior. This was possible for some of the bears more than others.

When the quarantine was lifted, we delighted in stripping the plywood boards off door nine, unveiling Bärle to the world again. She was excited, and crammed her right eye through the mesh to look down the hall. As she took deep, illuminating breaths, her nares flooded with juices, causing her to drool.

Breeding season was now an on-again, off-again proposition, and the other bears were moving in and out of libidinal fixation, changing almost hourly. Two days after Bärle's quarantine ended, Jewel, who had been camped out on the tundra, finally came inside, apparently less offended by Triton's existence, and we were able to give Bärle access to the enclosure.

Bärle walked through door nine, crossed the hall, and stepped out of door eight onto the tundra again—finally. It was a warm fifty degrees Fahrenheit, with plenty of snow still lying around in patches. Bärle meticulously went through the entire acre of tundra, smelling and lip- and tongue-checking grass, sticks, leaves, enrichment, and snow. She lay down in the snow and rubbed, rocked, and rolled until she was covered from nose to tail with tiny, frosty snowball dingleberries. Her foray lasted about five hours, and by the afternoon she had come back into her apartment and fallen asleep in her den nest.

For the next few days, we resumed giving Bärle and Sissy access to each other, separated only by the fence. As before, Bärle was fascinated and spent her time watching everything Sissy did. Sissy was peaceable to the point of being uninterested. According to this behavioral barometer, it was time.

On March 2, we fed Bärle and Sissy as much breakfast as they could possibly eat, including favorites like herring. Although all the bears' appetites had increased, they were still being picky about what they ate. We had been increasing their foods over the last few weeks to demonstrate that there was no shortage.

Bärle was anxious to go outside, and took her breakfast over to door nine to eat, possibly so that she wouldn't miss anything like the door opening or other bears walking by. Occasionally she paced perpendicular to the door in anticipation of going out. I joined her at the fence and put my head close to the mesh to greet her while she waited for the keepers to finish hyper-enriching the tundra enclosure. Gently she stuck the tip of her black nose through the metal weave and touched my nose. Having gotten my attention, she scurried over to door nine and performed a quick mock-pace toward it, illustrating that she wanted to go out. I understood.

When everything was in place, we gave Sissy access to the tundra. Bärle watched intently as Sissy passed door nine and disappeared through door eight. When Sissy was settled in on the far side of the tundra shredding a lunch bag, we opened door nine. Anticipating that Bärle might need some encouragement, I went over to sit with her in the hall, but she was out the door by the time I got there.

Bärle moved across the south side of the tundra in Sissy's direction and stopped briefly to consider Triton, who was standing across the moat eyeing her and surveying the proceedings. We repeatedly called to Sissy, trying to give her the heads-up on Bärle, but Sissy was completely engrossed in her lunch bag, digging through the straw for grapes, raisins, and peanuts—her favorites. For at least ten minutes, Bärle wandered about feigning interest in enrichment, sticks, rocks, grass, and snow while looking directly at Sissy.

Finally, she resolved to greet Sissy. In cub-like fashion, she walked straight up to Sissy and tried to touch the side of her face with her nose. Sissy whirled around and faced her off, clucking, huffing softly, and mock-mouthing Bärle's neck area, backing her up. Sissy was assertive and confident but not excessively aggressive. We had counted on her for a measured response, and we were not disappointed. Perhaps Sissy sensed Bärle's complete lack of malice, which is what I had experienced when she touched my nose to get my attention earlier that morning.

As undaunted as a bear cub, Bärle tried again to make contact, tobogganing on her side several times across the snow toward Sissy, asking her to play. It was hard for a human not to fall for the sweet little smile on her elfin bear face as she tried desperately to make a friend. Again, Sissy engaged her head on, moving forward and backing Bärle up while huffing in her ears and mock-biting. Bärle got the message and went about her fake foraging business while considering her options. Inexperienced in polite adult bear behavior, Bärle was not at all clandestine about watching Sissy but stared straight at her from wherever she was in the enclosure. Sissy ignored her. We knew Bärle's mind wasn't on foraging, since she was sorting through straw and eating Cheerios, which she normally ignored.

Throughout the rest of the day, Bärle either slid or amiably walked up to Sissy but was met with the same repelling response; on one occasion Sissy purposefully backed Bärle into the pool. Clearly, Sissy wanted to be left alone.

Technically, this integration had been a success. It was peaceable, and we had the beginning of a new group. But sadly, Bärle was still alone.

To give her some time to acclimate to each new bear, we planned for two-week intervals between introductions. Now was the time to give Bärle access to the facility's crown jewel, the 170,000-gallon, thirteen-foot-deep saltwater pool with visual access to the seals. On Bärle and Sissy's fifth day together, Bärle experienced her first deep water since she had swum with her mother in the Hudson Bay so long ago. She moved with missile precision across the pack ice enclosure and, after a hurried reconnaissance at the water's edge, waded into the pool, where she was enveloped by the cold water. Watching her, I could almost feel the layers of circus bear flotsam wash off her psyche, freeing her polar bear spirit after all of these years.

133

Any concerns I may have had about Bärle's swimming abilities vanished as she periodically tested the water's depth to find where the shoals gave way to the thirteen-foot pelagic end. In her first hour, she ate all of the fish we had thrown in and was enthralled to discover the people watching her through the poolside picture window of the Exploration Station. Seemingly testing its limitations, she pawed at the window in several places. Had she ever experienced glass before? It seemed unlikely. She got out and searched the pack ice for Sissy, who lay resting on her belly in the sun. Bärle moved within ten feet of Sissy and stared at her for several minutes, as if willing her to go swimming. Sissy ignored Bärle, as usual. Drawn like metal to a magnet, Bärle was back in the water a second time.

This time she swam to explore the deep end, effortlessly gliding through the water like an elegant manta ray over the heads of excited zoo visitors in the acrylic viewing tunnel beneath her. She reached the wall of thick acrylic viewing windows dividing the polar bears' pool from the 100,000-gallon saltwater seal pool. When the Arctic Ring of Life was first built, there was some concern about how the seals would deal with having one of their top predators living next door. Planners banked on the fact that seals are intelligent creatures and would realize that they were safe from the bears. Within a few hours, the seals understood that the bears could not get at them, and individuals from each species began to play tag with each other. Triton and Kiinaq (pronounced "Kee-nack"), a large young male gray seal, developed a play relationship, seeking each other out in the crowd. Sometimes Triton chased Kiinaq, and sometimes Kiinaq chased Triton.

In the deep end, Bärle was busy inspecting the underwater perimeter of the pool. Suddenly she froze upright in the water, looking like Wile E. Coyote about to be hit by an oncoming train; then she scurried behind one of the dividing pillars as Frieda the harbor seal nonchalantly swam on her back past the window. How Bärle had missed the seals' movement earlier I don't know, but they had her attention now. Hiding behind the pillar that she was hanging onto, Bärle stole furtive glances at the seal. She surfaced for air, submerged again like a stealthy submarine, and methodically checked the caulking on all four sides of the window. Bärle was hunting. Frieda continued cruising belly up on her usual route, blissfully indifferent to Bärle.

Bärle's attitude toward seals never changed. Seals were meant for hunting, and she spent hours keenly watching them and developing and perfecting hunting techniques—probably as a result of being reared by a wild mother. The other polar bears rarely stalked the seals and either developed play relationships with them or ignored them.

Icee, who was the next bear to be introduced to Bärle, had had a busy few weeks. She had moved into a final bout of cycling for the breeding season and had a pinkish, watery blood spot on her bottom, rubbed herself against the fencing as she walked by, and stimulated herself when she was alone. She twerked at Triton when he came inside the building and sought out the room next to his when the bears were brought inside for breakfast. Triton's appetite had increased, and he had stopped calling to the females, except for the days when Icee solicited his interest. Although Triton was her first breeding choice, she had access to Adak and bred with him while Triton challenged Adak from across the moat.

On March 16, the deep snowy patches had almost disappeared from the tundra. It was overcast and not too hot—just above freezing—good weather for polar bear introductions. We followed the usual introduction routine, bringing all of the bears inside for a large breakfast while we cleaned and distributed what seemed like a ton of enrichment foods and items on the tundra. This introduction was well timed; Sissy had been growing progressively less tolerant of Bärle's requests to play, snapping and growling at her. When it was time, we gave Icee access to the tundra first. Bärle had been pacing perpendicular to door nine, indicating that she wanted to go outside, a sentiment supported by Sissy, who was standing right behind her. Instead of going right out of door eight onto the tundra, Icee stopped in the hall at door nine and touched noses with Bärle through the mesh. Bärle pawed at the door, trying to open it. This was a good sign. As soon as Icee had plopped herself down with a lunch bag on top of the tundra cave hummock, we gave Bärle and Sissy access. Again I attempted to position myself near door nine to encourage Bärle if necessary, but again I got there in time to see Bärle's rear end disappear out the door, followed by Sissy's.

This was to be an active introduction from the beginning. Icee was on a walkabout, moving from lunch bags to branches to scatter feeds. Watching other bears, Bärle seemed to have learned that she was supposed to feign interest by food checking and doing other things, but she did a mediocre job and often looked directly at Icee. Within minutes Icee had traveled right up to Bärle and introduced herself. The two met nose to nose and immediately engaged in the traditional cheek-sniffing behavior. Each bear repeatedly smelled the other bear's face in the jowl area, most often where the jaw-bones connect, taking shallow breaths in rapid succession through the nose. A bear's world is about olfactory messaging—receiving and leaving scent. Their few active sweat glands, which happen to be situated in that area, may well serve a critical role as scent glands. Cheek-sniffing is so common in bear greetings that it is likely to be an important behavior.

The bears' cheek-sniffing evolved into open-mouthed fenc-ing and mock-biting each other's necks. Icee was a self-confident, often benevolent, and manipulative bear, qualities that seem to be common in wise older females, who work to maintain the group's peace. Both bears were gentle and relaxed, neither showed signs of trying to dominate the other, and both were smiling whenever their mouths were closed.

Eventually Icee moved off to investigate enrichment items. Bärle watched her go and then jumped into the pool, splashing and mucking about with submerged branches. Icee began walking the perimeter of the pool, and Bärle followed in the water. Icee then stationed herself facing Bärle and bopped her head up and down, seeming to insinuate that any second now she might jump in. She repeated this behavior several times and finally leapt on top of Bärle in a water-wrestling tumble.

Bears do not express meaningless behaviors any more than a human does. Icee's initial walk around the pool was similar to the oft-repeated food-asking demonstration in which a bear walks a full circle or semicircle around another bear's cache—to identify the desired object—and then touches that bear's muzzle to ask per-mission to eat some of the food.

Icee rarely had disagreements with the other bears. She was in the habit of exhibiting cordial bear behavior, and this was the key to her success. Icee and Bärle paw-splashed, hugged, mouth-fenced, wrestled, and held each other's head under water all morning.

Sissy, who had been keeping an eye on the playing pair for several hours while feeding, approached the pool and stood motionless, looking directly at Icee. I recognized that stern, smile-less, head-hanging, eyes-staring-over-the-lowered-muzzle, vulture-like look. Sissy was not happy, and it seemed that Icee was the cause. The water wrestling continued, but within a few minutes Icee exited the pool and greeted Sissy with a quick muzzle touch. Icee moved off to roll in the grass to dry off, and Sissy left the area to resume foraging. Bärle just stood there in the pool watching them—alone again. She slowly got out of the water, walked up to Icee, got her attention, and playfully took a few floppy steps back to the pool, looking over her shoulder. Icee did not follow. Bärle then tried to approach Sissy, who instantly bluff-charged her in a few lightning-quick steps. In a tactical error, Bärle turned to run, and Sissy shot forward and bit her on the rump. This seem-ingly over-the-top aggressive behavior put an end to Bärle's play invitations.

Despite this one strained encounter, the bears got along peace-ably for the rest of the week, mostly because Bärle left Sissy alone and came to understand that Icee was only interested in the occa-sional bout of water sports. A few days later, Sissy was moving slowly and did not seem well, vomiting and favoring her right rear leg. We monitored her carefully, but before we could consider taking any invasive action, Sissy's appetite and gait improved. As we continued to move out of breeding season, most of the bears were recovering their normal temperament—all but Jewel. She was seeking solitude more often, even away from Nikki at times. I worried about this behavior, but since the bears were still sub-ject to capricious hormonal fluctuations, it was difficult to identify her motivation. All we could do was respect her wishes whenever possible. Since Bärle was accommodating other bears well, we felt comfortable shortening the intermission between introductions to one week.

The only two bears left in Adak's group to be worked into the new group were Adak and Vilma. Since Vilma was known to be prickly, bossy, and domineering, we chose Adak as the next bear for integration. The introduction of a male could be challenging for Bärle, but the other females felt free to be casually assertive with him, suggesting that they considered him to be fairly benign. March 23 was another cool but sunny spring day. We had separated Icee and Sissy from Bärle so that she could watch who was going out onto the tundra and make a decision based on this knowledge. As was our routine, the bears were all fed breakfast while we cleaned and enriched the tundra enclosure. As was their routine, they inhaled the breakfast in a millisecond, since they were desperate to go outside, moaning, banging on doors with a back hand, huffing, pacing, showing pointy upper lips, jaw-snapping, and wide-mouth yawning—all signs of annoyance with the maid service.

Bärle watched from behind the mesh of door nine as Sissy and Icee went out onto the tundra first. Adak attempted to muzzle-greet Bärle through the mesh as he passed by, but she backed away. When the other bears were settled with enrichment on the tundra, I opened door nine and went over to the hall fenceline to keep Bärle company. She apprehensively moved into the hall and stayed there. I wasn't surprised. In the circus her approach to males had to have been a desperate balance between fortitude and survival instinct to ensure her preservation. Bärle methodically rubbed her face and body against the doorframes and walls, resolutely leaving an olfactory calling card, as wild bears do on rocks, trees, and other landforms. I have often observed especially feverish expressions of this behavior during an introduction when bears are tenuous about their position. The purpose of this behavior seems to be to strengthen the idea that they belong to this area—a bit like hanging up a shingle saying that the bear has a home here and some ownership of resources. After three minutes of scent-painting the walls, this little Braveheart went outside.

Bärle walked north of the cave hummock, feigning interest in scatter feeds and frequently looking about and sniffing the air, as if trying to locate Adak. She spotted him on the south side of the enclosure near the pool. When he saw her, Adak threw himself onto the ground, rocking and rolling, rubbing spring mud, fresh grass, twigs, and rotting leaves into his coat. It seems that he was hanging out a shingle of his own.

Adak had a particularly flat head, and for some reason his fur parted down the center of it, giving him a rather comical, geeky appearance from a human perspective. Between that, his rotund shape, and his filthy coat, he cut a goofy figure. When Bärle sat down near him to eat some treats, Adak immediately approached her and attempted his traditional less-than-elegant rump-seeking maneuver. Bärle stood up and spun around to thwart him. When Adak dropped to the ground and rolled onto his back for more gyrating in the dirt, Bärle slid forward on her belly in the grass toward him. Then she stood up and moved away—remarkably, with her back to him. Taking full advantage of the situation, Adak righted himself, quickly approached her, and stuck his nose into her rump. Again Bärle spun around and foiled his efforts.

For several hours the two alternated between feeding, muzzle-greetings, and Adak's dirt dance. This introduction was passing by so peaceably that I wondered if I was missing some subtle communication between the pair. Then, in the *pièce de résistance*, Bärle decided to take a noon-hour nap right in front of Adak. It was now official: six out of six female polar bears did not take Adak seriously as a viable male bear. Poor Adak! Bärle played with the blue ball in the pool for the rest of the afternoon by herself.

In the week that followed, Bärle treated Adak the same way the other female bears treated him. On one occasion Adak attempted to squeeze by her in the hallway. Bärle blocked his path, huffed, jaw-snapped, spit, and growled in his face so emphatically that he backed off and let her go first. But within minutes of this encounter, she let both Sissy and Icee bypass her.

Bärle also seemed to copy other behaviors. One morning, she chose to not come inside when we called but stayed outside with Sissy, who had initially refused to come in. This was a first, and it was a good sign of recovery. Bärle was learning that there were no negative consequences to not doing as she was requested. No one yelled at her, beat her, or otherwise abused her. She was not the first bear who wanted to do her own thing once in a while, and she wouldn't be the last. We took this behavior in stride and, as always, worked around it.

It was the morning of March 28, and if a layperson had entered the bear building, he would have thought that it was possessed by a very loud, very nasty spirit. This was Vilma's introduction day. Since it took extra time to clean and hyper-enrich the tundra, the bears had to wait a little longer than usual for outside access. Vilma had hoovered up her breakfast and now had to endure our snail-paced work. Her excruciatingly loud bovine-like bellows, amplified by the building's hall structure, could be heard by the staff at the far end of the tundra. In case we hadn't heard her the first time, Vilma indignantly paw-slammed the metal slides at intervals. I offered her some grapes to calm her down, but even she couldn't hear me over the din of her discordant sounds. She spotted my movement, flew to the fence, did a front-footed paw-stomp into the floor, and hissed a stream of hot, smelly fish breath into my face.

We were ready. The keepers came off the tundra, locked up the enclosure, and went inside. We realized that we'd have to de-escalate Vilma's behavior by letting her go outside first. If we hadn't known Vilma as well as we did, we might have reconsidered the day's mission. True to character, Vilma waddled quickly down the hall past Bärle and disappeared out door eight. Vilma immediately began checking enrichment, greeted Triton, who was watching from the pack ice across the moat, and then continued her foraging. Vilma had been alone all week since Adak's introduction to the new group. It was likely that she detected the change in our routine and anticipated that she would be introduced into the group that day. As always on introduction days, all staff members were present, a volunteer photographer was in the building, and massive amounts of enrichment were prepared.

The morning's drama did not seem to affect Bärle's spirit. I opened door nine, and Bärle was gone. She feigned interest in foraging as she moved about the enclosure, frequently lifting her head in reconnaissance. When she located Vilma's position, Bärle carefully ate her way over there. For the next fifteen minutes all was calm; it was like watching five very large grazing sheep. Then Vilma approached Bärle with the traditional cheek-sniffing and mouth-fencing. After a few amiable and low-key minutes, it became apparent that Vilma had an agenda. First she tried to corral Bärle into going west, toward the pool. Bärle sat down, so Vilma tried to nudge her from behind. When that didn't work, Vilma moved around to face Bärle and stuck her nose and head down Bärle's chest, trying to raise her to her feet. At first it wasn't apparent to Bärle—or me—what Vilma was doing, and she bolted a short distance. This move worked for Vilma, because now Bärle was facing west toward the pool, and again Vilma tried to push her in that direction.

Finally Bärle got the message and followed Vilma to the water. Immediately Vilma leapt in and splashed the water with both paws. Bärle just stood there staring at her. At first she had been smiling, but her smile waned as Vilma's splashing grew more intense and she slammed her entire upper torso onto the water, causing massive pool tsunamis. Bärle was drenched, as was everyone watching, including me. I shared Bärle's reticence. Vilma had lost her patience—again—and the intensity of her demonstration was worrisome. What could her motive be? Vilma's pointy upper lip of annoyance vanished when Bärle slowly entered the pool. Vilma moved into the deeper water in the center and porpoised in shallow dives in front of Bärle, who instantly copied her.

Both bears were smiling. They played for hours, eventually incorporating the big blue ball into the game. We learned something new about Vilma that day. Despite her often-abrasive personality, which may be why she was always left to play water polo alone, she seemed to desperately want someone to play with. These two very different bears forged a lifelong friendship based on this interest. And Bärle got what she needed—a bear friend who had her back.

8

FRIENDS WITH BENEFITS

Bärle Chooses a Mate

IN THE COURSE of my career there have been several times when life conspired with a storm of events so challenging that my only option was to dig in deep, stay in the moment, and rely on my emergency training to keep a cool head. The six weeks that followed Vilma's introduction to Bärle was such a time. Bärle was adjusting to her new circumstances, she had a playmate in Vilma, she treated Adak the same way the other females did, and Icee and Vilma looked after her interests. Bärle was fitting in with the girls, but instead of planning the next introduction, Bärle temporarily faded from our radar, and Sissy and Jewel moved to the forefront of immediate concern. Some of their behaviors seemed vaguely inconsistent with breeding season. It was subtle, something else was going on, and I had a bad feeling. We all felt the clouds gather.

There was an upwelling in breeding behavior again. Sissy was dripping pinkish blood droplets from her rear end. All signs of blood or bleeding anywhere on a bear was routinely reported to the veterinary team and was recorded. As usual, before we could determine exactly where the blood was coming from—vagina, anus, furry rump, or otherwise—Triton and Adak sniffed it out for us.

Both males now spent time near Sissy, Triton with fencing between himself and Sissy, and Adak trying to finagle a favorable position next to her. Sissy continued to maneuver around them by coming inside irregularly. The driblets disappeared within a day.

Jewel was also coming inside irregularly again. We were taking urine samples from both Sissy and Jewel by sucking up a specimen with a syringe from puddles on the floor in the morning when they did come in. Some of us sensed that both Sissy and Jewel were urinating less frequently and passing less liquid. This was a subjective observation, because the bears needed the freedom to come and go as they wished and we couldn't exactly run along behind them with a specimen bottle. We added this concern to the list of behaviors to be carefully monitored, but what were the odds that both bears had urination issues? We were already taking routine monthly stool samples from all of the bears and now added opportunistic urine sampling to the mix.

Jewel's vulva was swollen, another sign of cycling, but her gait seemed slightly skewed. Breeding females with a swollen vulva walk with a stiffer hind-legged gait and tend to spread their back legs a bit more. But Jewel's hind-end gait was so bowlegged that her toes appeared to be touching on each stride. Polar bears' front and back feet are normally pigeon-toed, perhaps as an evolutionary adaptation to help them better distribute their body weight on thin sea ice. Jewel's posture seemed extreme, however, and different from her normal gait when in breeding mode. Triton concurred with our diagnosis that Jewel was cycling again, and he began to court Jewel on the tundra and pack ice. She allowed him to corral her into various areas of her choice but at first did not allow breeding. She simply sat down. Possibly as a demonstration, Triton, massive as he was, periodically tried to lie on top of her like a blanket. It amazed me that she had the strength to handle his 758 pounds without being squashed flat as a pancake.

When Jewel did come inside, an astute keeper was able to spy an abscess through the fur on her rump. Jewel, Nikki, and Sissy had been having recurring hot spots since the inception of this prolonged breeding season in January. Since polar bears typically lose interest in food as they vie to mate, the bears normally lose a great deal of weight during the process, and we surmised that the hot spots might be caused by temporary nutritional deficiencies. We were also seeing an increase in small abscesses on Jewel and Sissy, which muddied the diagnostic waters. At the same time, in the rough and tumble of breeding season, it was normal for bears to incur cuts and scrapes that could become infected.

Three weeks after Vilma was introduced to Bärle, Triton and Adak confirmed that both Sissy and Jewel were cycling in a second upwelling. Sissy was again dripping blood from her hindquarters and sidestepping males, and Jewel was allowing Triton to breed her. Jewel appeared tired, and when she finally came inside, we called the vets to check her and kept her inside for overnight observation. After a day's rest and a prescribed course of antibiotics and pain relievers, Jewel seemed better and wanted to go outside again. As always, the question was, do you keep her inside for further observation, which would stress her, or do you give her access to the outdoors, which may help in her recovery but mean that you have lost temporary access to her? We let her out. Jewel's cure for what we thought was her still-sore rear end was to spend hours at a time lying with her rump in the shallow end of whatever pool she was near. At other times she floated in the deep end.

The medicines were difficult to get into her, since she had no appetite, a common occurrence in breeding season. She became a ghost bear, lying low and staying outside. Although Jewel had surges of energy, her bad days seemed to be outnumbering her good days. It was time to do a veterinary examination under anesthetic. Next time she came inside we would keep her in.

Things got worse. Jewel appeared to be retching, but there was nothing to vomit. She stood statue-still in the pool, neck deep in water, closing her eyes on and off. It would be dangerous to knock her down for a veterinary examination while she was outside, because she could drown in the pool or fall into the moat immediately after being darted. Within a few days, when she had recouped slightly and was moving around, we decided to put Icee and Vilma out with Jewel in the hopes that she would come in with them when we called. Jewel had constant access to the pool room, and when we came back from lunch, Jewel was in the pool in Bärle's old apartment! Overjoyed, we quietly and stealthily closed door nine.

May 10 was a very long and, sadly, unforgettable day. Sissy had also come in the day before. She ate some breakfast but immediately vomited. We kept her inside overnight as well. Both Sissy's and Jewel's urine specimens showed irregularities. We would knock down both bears so that we could take blood samples and skin biopsies. The veterinarians would also perform an abdominal ultrasound on Jewel.

Bärle, Vilma, Icee, and Adak were moved to the pack ice for the day. Nikki seemed unnerved during the abridged and speedy version of the morning feeding and cleaning routine. It hadn't escaped her notice that both her sister and her preferred companion had been kept in overnight. She tried to make contact with both before being sent out on the tundra with Triton.

Sissy's physical examination and blood work revealed that she was in complete renal failure. There was nothing we could do. Sissy was euthanized at the age of twenty-seven. We were stunned. One question immediately stabbed me: "What did I miss?" But we had to keep moving. Deflated, I carried on, as did the rest of the crew, some with tears in their eyes. We refocused. Jewel needed our complete attention.

Jewel's physical examination revealed another abscess, this one on her right rear paw, which we treated. Our veterinarian suspected, and the tests later confirmed, that Jewel had an infection—not just the abscess but something more serious. Our plan was now to keep her inside and accessible so that we could give her 100 percent of her antibiotic and pain reliever, something that was not possible when she was outside. She was slow to wake from the anesthesia and very tired. We stayed with her until late in the day. As I drove home, my mind raced over the plans for Jewel's treatment over the next few days, all the problems that could or would arise, and the possible solutions we could try on a moment's notice.

The sun was setting, and I let my thoughts rest on Sissy as I waited at the border to cross into Canada, where I lived. Sissy was the first bear I had bonded with shortly after I arrived at the Detroit Zoo, which was remarkable, since she was such a private bear.

She had had several molars extracted by the veterinarian, and the following morning had woken covered in a slimy, bloody salivary mess. Her medications from the day before had worn off, and she was stiff and in pain. While we waited for the veterinarian to come with her morning medications, I hooked up a garden hose and offered her a gentle cascade of warm water to drink if she wanted it. Instead she started to wash herself with it. She held her paw under the arch and let the fur soak up the water like a washcloth. She then gently rubbed her face, effectively washing off the pinkish goo from her muzzle. This method must not have been effective for washing an entire polar bear body because she then demonstrated the washing motion on her front right upper leg while maintaining eye contact with me and then gently slapped it in the traditional "right here, right now" bear demonstration. With some apprehension, I pointed the flow at her front right foot. Without moving her foot, she maintained eye contact with me and re-slapped her front right upper leg, this time displaying the pointy upper lip of annoyance. So I raised the hose to shoulder level, and she proceeded to rub her paw on her leg, effectively washing her leg.

148

Sissy slapped another body part and then another, and methodically washed each as I turned the stream on it. I was in the middle of one of the most comprehensive communication displays that I had ever experienced, and I didn't want to screw it up. So I was careful to follow her lead, with one exception. When she was washing her right hip, I thought a finer, diffused mist might work better, so I placed my thumb over the nozzle to create a lovely delicate spray. Sissy stopped washing and stared at me. Clearly I was wrong. What did I know about washing a polar bear body anyway? I sheepishly took my thumb off the nozzle. The water cascade resumed, and Sissy went about her washing business again.

The following day, I arrived at the zoo at sunrise. Jewel hadn't changed location since the day before, though she had changed position. This was not good. We tried to interest her in various foods, including savory roast chicken, but she was not interested. The veterinary technician came and, using a syringe pole, injected her with antibiotics and a pain reliever. Jewel was not particularly happy about that, but we had no choice.

The following morning, Jewel was standing and drinking from the automatic waterer when the keeper arrived. We were cautiously optimistic and hoping for a trend. After tending to the other bears and shifting them back outside, we opened door nine, hoping to entice Jewel down the hall and into a clean bedroom with a fresh straw bed and food. She went. We offered her roast chicken, a turkey leg, ham hocks, and polar bear chow bread with peanut butter. We tried an apple, a pear, a carrot, canned cat food, mackerel, and herring. Jewel ate nothing. This time we had to blow-dart her with the drugs because she was wise to our stick-poling ways and stood farther away from the fenceline. On the dart's impact, she furiously jump-stomped her front paws into the ground at us and exhaled a fuming, defiant breath of steam in protest. Good, she was feeling better!

Over the following days, Jewel moved from bedroom to bedroom, drinking from each automatic waterer. Her gait was slow and her back legs appeared wobbly at times, but this was an improvement. We continued to offer a daily buffet of food options, and although we never actually saw her eat, she was eating and defecating small amounts here and there. Six days into her drug regime, Jewel took a turn for the worse. Her energy waned, though she was eating more. On occasion she appeared to close her eyes while urinating.

On May 17, our veterinary team immobilized Jewel again and found her to be in kidney failure. Feeling that we could still offer her some quality of life with an appropriate diet and medication, we gave Jewel plenty of fluids and antibiotics. Although she woke from the anesthetic, she never moved more than her head and her legs. Jewel was euthanized on May 18, at the age of twenty-three, as a result of kidney failure. I felt flat, like a cardboard cutout. I stepped outside the building, just for a moment. I could hear the steady hum of traffic on Ten Mile Road. The clouds had gathered since the morning. A cool breeze was blowing in. I was cold.

In the aftermath of these arduous weeks, it was time to pick up the pieces. My staff threw themselves into cleaning the entire Arctic Ring of Life. Caring for two sick bears and dealing with breeding season and Bärle's rehabilitation had put us behind in our traditional spring-cleaning regime. We donned scuba gear and we scrubbed the saltwater pool, fire-hosed outdoor enclosures, bleached walls and floors, and dismantled, disinfected, and reorganized the kitchen. It was therapeutic for us all and allowed us some time to rethink Bärle's introduction plan.

150 Of all the bears, we surmised that Nikki had suffered the greatest loss, since both her sister and her best friend were gone. As had been so poignantly demonstrated over the previous six weeks, bears have a way of just soldiering on. Before Sissy's and Nikki's deaths, if I had been asked whether a bear would move into estrus when compromised by renal failure, I would have said no, that such a physically taxing condition might disrupt the normal reproductive process. And I would have been wrong. Sometimes there is simply no accounting for biology. Survival truly seems to be everything.

Now we wondered if Nikki or the other bears would show any signs of distress or behaviors that we might attribute to mourning. There was nothing, and yet there was something. It was difficult to pin down, but bear events all seemed to go well—too well. The height of breeding season was over, bears shifted in and out of the building as we needed them to, and there were no great arguments between bears over personal differences or property. Nikki, who was otherwise quite social, engaged in solitary activities much of the time, taking toys like the brown bobbin from the building with her outside to play with by herself.

At our monthly polar bear weigh-in, Triton's, Adak's, and Vilma's weight had gone up, coinciding with their appetite increases and corroborating our conclusions about breeding behavior. Triton, who often stayed behind in the morning to finish everyone else's breakfast leftovers, had gained a whopping seventy-four pounds over just a few weeks. Nikki and Icee had not gained weight, but Bärle had lost a worrying thirty-one pounds. We hoped it was related to the changes that had taken place.

To ultimately integrate Triton into Bärle's group, we first had to reintroduce Triton and Nikki to Icee and Vilma. Triton and Icee quickly paired up like the old companions they were and traveled, ate, and slept together. Vilma simply greeted Triton with several cheek-sniffs and then busied herself playing solitary water polo. Temporarily alone with Adak, Bärle was not happy and began to pace. Realizing our mistake, we quickly gave Vilma access to Bärle, and the two friends were back at their endless game of water polo.

On June 15, we loaded the tundra with enrichment items and fed the bears an enormous breakfast in the building in preparation for Nikki's introduction to Bärle. Bärle watched from behind the mesh of door nine as Adak, Vilma, and Nikki walked past her in the hall and went outside through door eight. She anxiously took small walking steps meant for our edification toward the door. Trying to comply, we could barely get door nine open as she impatiently squeezed through it to get out. The introduction was utterly anticlimactic. Although we had no behavioral information to suggest that the introduction would not go well, I had not anticipated this outcome. Bärle and Nikki looked at each other as if they had been together for years. Both were engrossed in investigating the enrichment items, swimming, and rolling in the grass.

In the afternoon, Adak stole the public's attention by rolling in the dirt again, as seemed to be his custom for introductions, and came up looking like a brown bear. No one would have guessed that two bears were being introduced. On the following day, Nikki greeted Bärle with several friendly cheek-sniffs, which Bärle reciprocated, and each moved on to other business. Bärle was behaving like a self-confident adult bear.

We were back to our normal routine of allowing the female bears to go with whichever male or females they wished in the morning, with the exception of Bärle and Triton. If a bear wanted to change enclosure halfway through the day, then she just needed to show up at the door when the keepers returned from the seal building around noon. Sometimes no bears were at the doors.

Sometimes a crowd of belligerent bears were at the doors. And sometimes a bear who was just kidding showed up at the door, walking halfway through it when the keeper opened it and then backing out at the last minute, running away in a floppy, playful gait or sticking his paw in the doorframe to foil the keeper's attempts at closing it. It was time to complete the integrations.

152

Rain pelted down on my car as I drove to work in the early morning of July 11—not what I was hoping for. Bärle's introduction to Triton was the grand finale of our integration odyssey. I hadn't slept much, restlessly going over and over plan A, then B, then C, and so on for the coming day. Each bear was an individual, and in making any decision we had to take into account the personal likes, dislikes, and issues of all of the bears. We had to be able to change plans, tactics, and direction at a moment's notice in triage fashion. Of all the introductions we had orchestrated for Bärle, I believed this one would be her greatest challenge. Fortunately, the bears were in the meet-and-greet mode that followed the frenzy of breeding season. But Triton was supersized next to Bärle; his head alone was twice the size of hers. At the last weigh-in he had gained 102 pounds in four weeks—a seasonally normal weight gain for a young male—and was now 934 pounds. Bärle too was gaining weight as we had hoped she would, but she was still just 450 pounds. She would have to rely on her newly acquired understanding of bear behavior to negotiate with Triton.

We brought all of the bears inside for a hearty breakfast of chow, herring, and trout. Although Nikki was socializing with the other bears, she was still spending substantial amounts of time by herself and likely would not appreciate being in the middle of the Triton and Bärle introduction. So Nikki was sent out onto the pack ice with Adak for the day. The bears knew the drill when they saw that we were preparing twice the regular amount of enrichment and food for the tundra enclosure. We carried out five-gallon bucket after five-gallon bucket of chow, fruits, vegetables, fish, and chicken and set ice treats afloat in the pool, along with Vilma and Bärle's favorite blue ball. Betsie Meister had harvested armfuls of fresh, leafy silver maple branches—Triton's favorite—and strategically placed them on the tundra. Then she dragged several whole saplings in and crammed them into the ten- foot-tall, stone inuksuk, which was meant as a cultural prop but served nicely as an enrichment station for the bears. It took us one and a half hours to fully load the tundra with enrichment.

It was time. The bears had been ready to go fifteen minutes after they had come in, which is how long it took them to inhale breakfast. Bärle was in the pool room, taking illustrative steps toward door nine. She watched as we opened door eight and gave Vilma and Icee access to the tundra. Then we gave Triton access. He walked past door nine and tried to greet Bärle with a sniff-check on his way out, but she backed away several feet and watched him leave. Within a few minutes I got the radio call that Triton was busy outside by the inuksuk, browsing on silver maple. I closed the mesh gate to the rest of the hall, opened door nine, and turned off the noisy hydraulic system. Suddenly it was quiet, except for the distant choir of a dozen house sparrows twittering in the rafters. Bärle didn't move. I crouched down on the hall floor to keep her company, and we both stared out of door eight. I could feel a warm summer breeze on my face. Bärle flared the wings of her nares, took long, deep breaths through her nose, and exhaled through her mouth, collecting information. All at once she busily rubbed her cheeks and body against the doorframe, the walls, and the mesh gate in a flurry of activity. She was nervous, and this decision took courage. Every large male she had encountered had been anxious, stressed, and often aggressive. I tried to speak in soft, encouraging tones: "Such a good girl, Bärle." She was taking her time. After ten minutes, this self-reliant little bear resolved to step outside.

Bärle was cautious, sniffing the air and searching for Triton as she crossed the tundra, periodically stopping to pretend to investigate enrichment. She alternated taking side-glances at Triton, who was still munching at the inuksuk, with looking straight at him. When he looked up she averted her eyes as if something elsewhere had caught her attention. Triton did the same, feigning lack of interest, and diverted his eyes when caught gazing at her. Then, remarkably, she turned her back to him, just as she had done with Adak. My heart rate sped up. I had no idea how to evaluate this. Was she being too nonchalant? Triton pretended to eat his way over to Bärle and took the last thirty feet in three giant leaps. Instantly they connected. Bärle twirled around to intercept him, and he tried to cheek-sniff her. She reared up and bounced off him, paw-punching him in the shoulder. He backed up. I was relieved— he was responsive. If she had been truly angry, she would have swiped at his head with her paw pad. A shoulder punch meant "back up".

Vilma and Icee both watched from a distance while pretending to eat. Each bear had a vested interest in a peaceable outcome. Triton and Bärle were key players in the group.

Triton moved forward, and again they danced like prizefighters. Both cheek-sniffed and huffed, showing that they were anxious, and Bärle pointed her upper lip. Drool was flying and they mouth-fenced. Bärle sat down, stood up, and backed up a few steps, while Triton stayed where he was. Bärle moved forward and engaged him. When he tried to flank her, she sat down.

The rain had stopped. A few seconds passed. Like lightning, Triton moved forward and mock-bit Bärle's neck. She flew at him, growled, and punched him in the shoulder again. My heart was pumping. Triton tried rump-seeking again, but she sat down. Triton moved off, hanging his head. Bärle reopened negotiations by moving closer to him. And suddenly Triton had a bright idea. With

154

his mouth he picked up a maple branch that had already been stripped of juicy leaves and dropped it in front of Bärle as a gift. She ignored it, walked over it, and sat down to foil any rump-seeking maneuvers. I detected a slight smile on her face. Triton left.

When attempting to understand the meaning of an animal's behavior, I find it's always helpful to observe how the other animals in the group interpret that event. Vilma and Icee had relaxed and refocused their attention on dissecting and devouring treats. I could stand down a bit. In short order Triton returned, dragging an entire maple sapling in his mouth, complete with leaves that he then dropped in front of Bärle. We were trying not to laugh with delight. Although Bärle was smiling, she moved away slightly, with her side to the tree, and looked in the opposite direction, ignoring the gift. Triton picked it up and put it down closer to her. Again she pretended not to see it. Insistently, he picked it up a third and fourth time and dropped it down next to her. On the fifth time he crashed it down right next to her, and Bärle accepted the gift with a quick sniff and lip-check. She turned and walked away, and he followed in traditional courtship behavior. Continuing the dance, she turned and halfheartedly chased him off.

Now Icee cut in and sought Triton's attention by greeting him nose to nose. Triton momentarily gave Icee his attention, leaving Bärle to just stand there and watch. My heart pounded again. Bärle turned to walk away but looked over her shoulder, beckoning him to follow. Triton looked from one female to the other. Icee huffed softly at him. When he turned to look at Icee, Bärle flew in his face and admonished him. Icee left, and Triton wisely feigned interest in grass. Bärle followed Icee partway up the path, then stopped, seemed to reconsider, and left to go swimming and play with the blue ball. Triton tried to join her, but she placed herself between him and the ball and lowered her head in annoyance, as if guarding the ball. Triton backed off and sat in the tall grass watching.

Bärle moved away from the pool and rolled in the grass to dry off. What happened next was unclear. Icee approached Bärle, there was a lightning-fast quarrel, and they separated.

Given the bears' personalities, it makes sense to me that Icee would have approached Bärle to make peace and that Bärle, in competition for Triton's attention, would have thwarted her overtures and growled at her. Icee's approach to Bärle had seemed relaxed and nonaggressive. I have learned over time and with experience that communication between polar bears is often so subtle that it is difficult for humans to discern who did what to whom and why.

Vilma wandered over to the pool to lie down, and Triton moved over to greet her briefly with a cheek-sniff while looking at Bärle. In traditional Vilma behavior, she reciprocated but did not bother to get up and seemingly ignored Triton. Both bears were looking at Bärle during this interaction. Considering that bears lock and maintain eye contact when they communicate, this behavioral sequence gave the impression that they were either asking for approval from Bärle or demonstrating a lack of interest in courtship behavior with each other. Vilma was frequently convincing at conveying an aloof indifference. Whether Triton and Vilma were asking for approval or showing indifference, Bärle allowed it without intervening.

The integrations were complete, and they had been successful. Bärle was leaving her life as a traumatized, naïve little circus bear in the dust, and had carved out a place for herself negotiating with our other self-concerned, opinionated, well-adjusted mature bears. She was a robust contender to be bartered with in normal bear negotiations.

The following day, we thought it best to put Icee with Adak and Nikki in the pack ice enclosure, just to give Bärle and Triton some time to interact without interference. They spent much of the day getting to know each other as they played in the pool. Periodically, Icee would watch them from across the moat on the pack ice. We felt a little sorry for Icee because she was not used to sharing Triton's attention, but bears are polygamous creatures and this was a natural course of events. We also felt a little sorry for Vilma, because she had lost sole custody rights over Bärle's pool-playing time.

Over the winter, Bärle and Triton developed an extraordinarily strong bond. They played together, slept together, ate together, and were frequently near each other. Their relationship became known locally, and crowds watched as they wrestled, oblivious to their adoring public. They were easily recognizable, since Triton was twice Bärle's height when they reared up on their hind legs to attack and counterattack in the shallow freshwater pool. Bärle used Vilma's upper-torso body slam to thoroughly soak Triton. Wild play sessions were interspersed with time-outs, when Triton would shake gallons of excess water off his coat, often casting oceans of water onto bystanders. He had steadily been gaining weight since breeding and now weighed in at 1,045 pounds. Bärle had also gained weight and was up to five hundred pounds. Triton was gentle and sensitive to Bärle's physical abilities, and he skillfully self-handicapped so as not to injure her.

One afternoon, they had been swimming in the saltwater pool in the pack ice enclosure, and Bärle was lying like a sphinx near the water's edge, watching Triton. From the pool, he stretched his upper torso across the deck and picked up a small, treat-loaded, PVC feeder in his mouth. Then he dog-paddled over to Bärle and dropped it under her nose. Smiling broadly, Bärle picked it up and placed it between her paws. Their eyes were locked in communication for the duration of the event. Triton was a gift-giver even

outside of breeding season. Their relationship was close and playful, and judging by their never-ending smiles, it was enjoyable.
Triton also paid attention to Icee when given the opportunity, and
this was sometimes accepted by Bärle and sometimes not. It was
all normal and natural and well within the social parameters of
polar bear behavior as I had come to understand it.

In September and October, breeding behavior started all over
again. It was subtle, but we sensed each bear becoming an island of
mood swings and daily—sometimes hourly—fluctuations of likes
and dislikes. Appetites waxed and waned. Some bears were slow to
go outside, and others were slow to come inside. Short outbursts
erupted between old friends but were settled or forgotten as the
same bears ate and slept together ten minutes later. The swings
intensified, becoming acute by December. We separated the bears
into groups for the breeding season. Triton was with Bärle and
Nikki, and Adak was with Vilma and Icee. The objective was to
allow Bärle to breed with Triton now that she was physically and
mentally strong.

As the season progressed, Triton actively courted Bärle, and
she allowed him to corral her into various areas of the tundra and
pack ice enclosures. She also grew progressively more intolerant
of Nikki, chasing her around periodically and huffing in her face.
Clearly Bärle was able to handle Triton on her own and didn't care
to have other females around. We gave Nikki access to Adak's group,
where she blended into the crowd when she chose to.

In January and February 2004, visitors, docents, and staff
observed breeding between Triton and Bärle. They were frequently
together, rubbing against each other, playing together, and sharing
food. Over time, Triton's attention naturally wandered to Icee, who
had been watching the romantic overtures from across the moat.
She too was cycling, and much to Triton's annoyance, she occasionally bred with Adak. In between trysts with Bärle, Triton wandered

up and down, following the moat wall and moaning so loudly he could be heard in the neighborhood, calling to Icee. According to his clock, it was time to move on, but this move was far different from what he was expecting.

Sadly, in accordance with the AZA Polar Bear Species Survival Plan, Triton was scheduled to move to the Indianapolis Zoo on March 29 to breed with an eighteen- year-old female bear named Tundra. This move proved to be exceptionally difficult for him. The Arctic Ring of Life offered larger, more complex enclosures, better husbandry possibilities, and more choices in social interactions than his new environment. Triton and Tundra did not do well together, and this socially oriented male bear became a loner, spending much of his time in repetitive swimming or pacing behaviors or lethargy. Tom Roy, a longtime docent at the Detroit Zoo whose voice Triton knew well, visited him in his new home. Roy called Triton's name repeatedly while he lay resting on the cement, but there was no response. Then Roy called Icee's name. Immediately, says Roy, "Triton's head shot up and he looked around."[1] Triton never truly acclimated to this new environment.

Zoos recognize that being constantly uprooted from one zoo environment and taken to another is stressful and frequently detrimental to bears, and they are testing an alternative solution for breeding. To maintain polar bears in North American zoos in low-stress, appropriate environments and compatible social groups, a twenty-two-year-old female polar bear at the Seneca Park Zoo named Aurora was artificially inseminated in January 2012. By February 2013, it was apparent that she was not expecting.

The procedure does show promise, however. In March 2012, two female polar bear cubs were reportedly born to an artificially inseminated mother in Tianjin, China. The cubs were taken from their mother and hand-raised by zoo staff, following a similar procedure used to raise dozens of giant panda cubs also born to artificially inseminated mothers in China. Since much invaluable maternal teaching is lost when cubs are raised by humans, zoo researchers chose Aurora as a good candidate for artificial insemination because she had skillfully and successfully raised four cubs.

In Triton's absence, we no longer had to manage two groups, since Adak was now the only male bear. For most of June, the bears were free to choose whichever enclosure or other bears they wished. Forgoing the fanfare of time-consuming courtship, Adak seized the day and bred with Bärle, who briefly allowed him to do so.

In a twist of fate so syncretic that it could only happen in real life, Triton's father, Norton, was sent from the Roger Williams Park Zoo in Rhode Island to live at the Arctic Ring of Life while his old enclosure was being refurbished. Triton's mother, Trixie, stayed behind in Rhode Island.

Norton was an enormous bear with the traditional Roman nose that many male polar bears possess. Triton had inherited Norton's 1,100-pound physique and—it was said—he got his good looks from his mother. Norton was another bear without a past. He was thought to have been born in December 1987 in the wilds of Alaska. How he came to be an orphan and end up in Anchorage as a yearling was unknown. He had lived peaceably for the last fifteen years with Trixie, a captive-born female polar bear at the Roger Williams Park Zoo. Norton had sired two cubs with her, one of whom was Triton.

Norton was known to be a very relaxed bear because his physical movements were most often quite slow, until he met Bärle. For most of June, Norton had visual access to Bärle and Vilma. Vilma greeted him in her traditional manner, with a quick cheek-sniff, and then ignored him. Bärle spent time at the mesh gates allowing him to cheek- and neck-sniff her, and she graciously reciprocated. Other times she simply ignored him. On June 28, Norton was introduced to Bärle and Vilma. Bärle made her confidence and self-regard known. She bluff-charged him twice when he approached. He responded well and held back. On one occasion she backed away from him into the building, as if uncomfortable turning her back to him. That was worrisome.

With time, she invited him to follow her by walking away and stopping to glance back at him. Norton followed. Vilma went about her foraging business but kept an eye on the proceedings. It was unclear whose idea it was, but the couple ended up in the moat. Bärle had allowed it. The two stood there for long periods of time looking at each other or relaxing by lying down and looking at each other. As the courtship dance progressed, they were eventually inseparable for a time. With two males, the females were again given options for which male and enclosure they preferred.

The summer passed, and Bärle grew less and less interested in social behavior and began to check dens and old nesting sites. On September 19, she was given exclusive access to the tundra enclosure and the pool stall and maternity den apartment. The hall gate was closed off and boarded up to create a visual barrier so that the other bears could not disturb her. There was a moratorium on noise, and only zookeepers and veterinary staff were allowed in the building.

Bärle was in her element. Like her mother before her, she moved from denning possibility to denning possibility. There were two sites that might be deemed appropriate in an expectant bear's eye—the cave under the knoll on the tundra and the cubbing den in the apartment. Everyone hoped she would choose the cubbing den in the building because it was equipped with cameras and staff could monitor her progress and adjust the temperature. To make that option more appealing, all of the straw was removed from the cave, and a giant fresh bed of straw was set up in the cubbing den.

162   At times, Bärle spent a few nail-biting hours resting in the cave, possibly testing it. If she had wanted to, she could easily have taken the straw out of the cubbing den and made a bed in the cave, but she didn't. She set up her own daily routine, and staff worked around it.

In early October Bärle slept in several places, such as the pool room, the transfer hall from the pool room to the den, and sometimes in the den itself. She was up at seven thirty in the morning when the staff arrived, and would eat a bite here and there, go outside for a short while, and then return to rest in the apartment. In her absence, the keepers opportunistically cleaned up what fecal material there was and replaced any urine-soaked straw. By late October Bärle was taking only a small bite out of each fish given her, but she still enjoyed leaf lettuce, which she had liked since her arrival. Boris and Kenny, Willie and Masha, and Alaska's caregivers reported the same preference from their charges, possibly because they had been fed a great deal of lettuce in the circus and possibly because the leafy greens provided much-needed hydration to quench their thirst; the bears had had only intermittent access to clean water. In keeping with our motto, "What Bärle wants, Bärle gets," several types of lettuce were ordered for her.

By early November Bärle was resting most of the day and only getting up on occasion. There were no more forays outside to the tundra. She began nest building in earnest, fluffing, rearranging, and then rearranging again the straw bed in the den. By mid-November she slept almost exclusively in the cubbing den. It was time.

9

TEACHING LIFE SKILLS
TO A POLAR BEAR

Bärle Raises Talini

NOVEMBER 22, 2004, was a beautiful fall day, sunny and just above freezing. But this did not matter to Bärle, nestled deep inside her den cocoon. She was slow to get up in the morning. The keepers had been offering her a small daily breakfast of fish, polar bear chow bread, and leafy greens in the transfer that connected the cubbing den to the pool room, just to maintain some contact. Bärle wasn't interested in food, and after greeting the keeper with a tired gaze, she went straight back to her nest.

The other bears had come and gone. They were their usual noisy, bustling selves, playing musical rooms as they jostled for breakfast and companionship while the pack ice and tundra enclosures were being serviced. Bärle could only hear the muffled sounds of their voices, their shuffling, and the hydraulic doors. Soon these kinetic characters were all scooted back outside by the keepers' shushing and shooing them in raised hushed tones. It was quiet again.

Bärle was restless but operating in slow motion. She scratched and licked her paws. She gently rearranged the straw in her nest. She came out and rested on her back in the transfer for a while. Then she went back into the den. She raked stray bits of straw together. She lay down in the nest, then changed to a sitting position. Soon she was back up and out into the transfer. Then she moved back into the den and fluffed the straw by flipping it like a flapjack, using her paw as a spatula. Such aimless, mildly agitated behavior continued all day.

By late afternoon the sun was setting, and a gentle twilight settled over the den. Bärle rested on and off, constantly changing position. Darkness drew in, enveloping her as it had her mother when she was denning in the wilds of the Hudson Bay.

At 11:06 PM, Bärle raised her hindquarters from her lying position and with her head down began breathing heavily in short, quick contractions. Two minutes later, a small, gooey pinkish-white cub dropped into the straw. Within minutes Bärle had reoriented herself and was smell-checking and licking parts of the amniotic sac off the cub. Thirty minutes later she gently picked the baby up in her mouth and carried her while rearranging straw and changing position. Bärle cradled the cub in the crux of her arm as she continued to lick her clean and dry her with her tongue, which was so big that it blanketed the baby each time.

By one thirty in the morning, the cub was sprawling on Bärle's chest, possibly nursing; it was difficult to tell exactly what was going on from the video. Finally, at 4:00 AM, it was confirmed on camera that the cub was nursing in on-again, off-again sessions that lasted until 4:45. Bärle was completely adept at and appeared confident in her nurturing skills. Staff could breathe a collective yet guarded sigh of relief. By 5:00 AM the cub was again licked clean and dry after nursing, and again Bärle changed their position out of view of the camera.

Around seven thirty in the morning, heedful of the baby's whereabouts, Bärle quietly stood up, left the baby in the straw, and briefly greeted the keeper in the transfer. After less than a minute, she disappeared back into the den. I have frequently observed these short forays and presume the mother is stretching, getting a breath of air, and possibly reassessing the safety of her environment. On these quick excursions, Bärle sometimes covered the cub in straw before she left, sometimes not, likely adjusting her behavior according to the ambient den temperature. For the next week, Bärle's days and nights were a routine of nursing the cub, licking the cub clean and dry, cradling the cub off the cold ground, sleeping with the cub, and taking the occasional short junket to the transfer.

Mentally and physically healthy polar bears are known to be attentive and patient mothers. In the wild they have been observed to adopt cubs for apparently altruistic reasons. In a long-term scientific study on Hopen Island in the Norwegian Barents Sea, a seven-year-old wild female with two four-month-old female cubs was immobilized and collared with a satellite telemetry device to monitor her movements after she was released and her cubs were given ear tags. Three days later, another seven-year-old female was immobilized within one hundred yards of the previous family. This female had three cubs, two males and one female. The female cub was immediately recognized by her ear tag as one of the two cubs from the first family studied. The research team was unable to determine what the circumstances of the adoption might have been, because any bear tracks had been erased by blowing snow. A hypothesis that the two mothers were related, rendering the adoption genetically self-serving, was laid to rest using microsatellite markers to determine relatedness. The mothers were genetically shown to not be related to each other, and the female cub was proven to not be related to the adoptive mother.

Oddly, it was postulated in the research paper that the adoption was due to mistaken identity. Being intimately familiar with the intellectual capabilities of polar bears, I reject that notion. It's clear that any bear mother can understand the difference between originally possessing two male cubs and suddenly possessing two male cubs and a female cub. It is in every way energetically more taxing and in no way beneficial for her to take on a third cub; thus, I propose that she adopted the third cub in an act of altruism. In addition, I continue to find it surprising that altruism is somehow considered unique to humans and that we believe genetic self-interest or lack of mental dexterity is the only way that animals preserve their own species.

Mother bears are known to be fiercely protective of their own cubs. They are not known to run off and fiercely protect the cubs of another female bear who happens to be grazing at the same berry patch. A few years ago I was observing numerous female bears with various cubs in tow feeding at a large berry patch on a south-facing mountain slope in Glacier National Park. There was a sound, or movement, or something, that I did not detect, but many of the bears on the slope suddenly stood alert. Instantly, several mothers huffed to their cubs to come and the females moved to stand in front of them, sandwiching the young between their hindquarters and the bushes. It was unnerving.

Looking in the direction that the bears were staring, I wondered who or what I was missing. I had made my presence known at the feeding ground from the beginning and had been accepted and then ignored. A few cubs whose mothers were not easily discernible to me were left unprotected by an adult. At no time did any of the otherwise protective females show any inclination toward protecting the seemingly unsupervised cubs. If a female can tell her cubs apart from others in that instance, she can certainly tell the difference in an adoption situation that will tap into her life-giving resources.

Although the daily duties of infant cub care are the same day after day—eat, clean, sleep; eat, clean, sleep; and so on—I have found that mothers and cubs are unique in their relationship and interactions. Some mothers appear nervous, constantly checking and moving their young; they seem agitated by crying and wiggling cubs; and they adjust and readjust the nesting material. Other mothers appear more confident and relaxed and are attentive when cubs cry but provide solutions that make the crying stop. Some cubs are very vocal and wiggle a great deal, and others are intermittently vocal and settle down when their mother feeds, cleans, or moves them.

Bärle proved to be a relaxed and confident mother. Her responses to the cub's cries were measured and often ended the crying. The cub, though very loud, did not cry long or often.

A polar bear cub's cry is similar to a human baby's cry and may be expressed by a myriad of notes and combinations of notes; you can find many recordings of the cries of infant bears, including polar bears, on YouTube. Bears of all species have an epipharyngeal pouch, roughly at the back of the throat, that is thought to be responsible for amplifying some of the communication sounds they make. It seems plausible that cubs put that intensifying chamber to good use in their often-screaming cries for service. It's possible that subadult and adult bears also use the pouch to make the clucking noise that seems to come from the back of the throat; it sounds like a bass version of human tongue clucking. I have heard the cluck used in a variety of circumstances to communicate agitation.

The often-loud, rhythmically pulsating sound uttered by nursing cubs is frequently described by bear keepers as "motor boating" or "machine gunning," both of which are accurate descriptive terms but somehow do not capture the serenity of a mother nurturing her cub. In the scientific literature, the sound has been described as humming or buzzing, which may be better descriptions but does not accurately portray the palpitations of the sound. YouTube also contains many recordings of this protracted neighing of nursing infant polar bears.

I have heard various species of female bears softly hum a single note or multiple notes during nursing. The most melodic of these, in my opinion, is that of spectacled bears, because they vary their song between multiple notes. Other species of bears may also hum in multiple notes, but I have not heard such songs and cannot find reference to them. A small female adult spectacled bear, the size of a German shepherd, named Melanka, who lived for some time at the Calgary Zoo, would hum, sometimes loudly, when she was nest building. Her humming was interspersed with soft huffs, clucks, and vocalizations that sounded as if she was lost in her thoughts and talking to herself.

The first week of Bärle's motherhood was a time of discovery by trial and error. For example, she would try to adjust the cub's position on her chest to suckle. Infant cubs are roughly the shape of a kielbasa sausage, with the addition of four flailing limbs. Their main mode of transportation is unintentional rolling from a higher place to a lower place. So when the baby rolled off Bärle's body, Bärle would retrieve her by gently mouth-grabbing the cub by her head, her feet, or her hind end. It was delicate work. Once back on her mother's body, the cub would crawl by instinct, searching for a milky, wet teat. Whatever one might think of the process, it worked.

Bärle also seemed to experiment with lying positions in the nest that would work for both mother and cub. There was much fluffing, poofing, and raking of straw while she kept an eye on her baby, and then she would lie down and position the cub. She settled on two primary positions—one, fortunately facing the camera, with the cub cradled in her paws or in the crux of her arm, and the second with her body curled around the cub with her back to the camera. On occasion Bärle would roll over onto her cub in her sleep, at which point the cub would squeal, if she could. Bärle always woke immediately, dug the cub out of the straw, and repositioned herself and the cub. Once, rather comically, Bärle accidentally sent the cub flying into the straw as she moved her paw. Bärle quickly retrieved the cub and reorganized them both. It was a good thing their straw bed was huge and deep. Keepers often left fresh straw out for her in the transfer, and Bärle would rake out the soiled straw with her claws and rebuild her nest with the fresh.

At the age of thirty-nine days, the cub opened her eyes and blinked. She also yawned for the first time on record and seemed to have grown. Rolling around was still a problem, however. Once she rolled off her mother's chest and bumped her head on the wall. Bärle carefully picked her up by the scruff of the neck, because now she had one, and licked her little noggin. On her forty-fourth day, the cub lifted her body and elevated her crawl to a walk. She took four steps, rested, and then took three more steps. On the next day, her ears stuck out much more prominently than they had before and appeared to be more developed. She also seemed to purposefully latch onto a teat as opposed to using the on-again, off-again approach of an infant. There were daily changes from incidental behavior to what appeared to be intentional gestures. She seemed to purposefully scratch her head, and she stretched and adjusted her body position.

She had her drop-dead adorable behaviors too. On one occasion she had the hiccups, which rocked her whole little wiener-shaped body. On another occasion she sat up for the first time and then fell over to the side. She took more wobble-walking steps between rolling and crawling and once migrated three feet within two minutes. Bärle had to be even more vigilant now because baby was on the move.

Aimless migration from the nest into walls, other rooms, under the straw, and into her mother's various body parts—which required Bärle's constant retrieval—evolved into following behavior. This behavior still required maternal attention, but not as much as the cub's previous adventures.

On the cub's sixty-seventh day, there was an interesting exchange between mother and cub. As was her habit, Bärle had left the cub in the den to go into the transfer for a break. The cub migrated over to the threshold between the two rooms. Bärle got up, picked up the cub in her mouth as if to move her back into the den, but then, as if she had changed her mind, put the cub back down again. Within seconds she repeated the behavior, but finally settled on leaving the cub where she was. From that day forward the cub was allowed to follow Bärle into the transfer and was officially introduced to the keepers one by one as they were scheduled to work with her.

Within the next few days there were other changes. The cub would stand on her hind legs against her mother to get Bärle's attention or to investigate something she had. Bärle also allowed the cub to lie next to her in the nest instead of on top of her, suggesting that the cub could now sometimes maintain her own body temperature without her mother's help.

At eleven weeks, the cub began to mouth Bärle's food, trying to bite first a piece of pear and then a fish head. Fearing that she might choke, the keepers concocted a bear baby food made of polar bear chow and cooked vegetation mush and presented it to mother and cub. Apparently this was not exactly a culinary delight: Bärle stopped eating. If mother stopped eating, the cub would stop eating too, so chunks of well-cooked, soft foods like yams, which Bärle enjoyed, were served up with mush on the side.

Thirteen weeks after giving birth, Bärle pawed at the mesh door asking to have access to the pool room in her apartment. It had been closed off while the cub was an infant because she could easily kill herself by falling into either an empty or a full pool. Bärle went straight into the pool for a long-awaited wash and found it empty. She escorted the cub down and back up the pool stairs. Each step was roughly the same height as the cub, turning this into an Olympic event for the little one. As the keepers were ushering them down the hall and out to the tundra, the other polar bears detected bear activity in the pool room. One of them was pounding on door eight to get back inside to further investigate. Bärle curtly huffed distress calls at the cub and pushed her toward the transfer. But the cub didn't want to leave and tried to dodge back around her mother. On the fly, Bärle grabbed the baby by the rump and dragged her into the transfer, then effectively corked the entrance with her body.

The cub was clearly starting to develop her own will. Feeding alongside her mother, the little bandit tried to make off with a giant carrot from under Bärle's nose by dragging it, since it was too heavy to carry. Bärle patiently reached over, picked it up with her mouth, and put it back in her own food pile.

Wild bear mothers gradually increase the difficulty of the challenges they introduce their cubs to. Although Bärle would likely have loved to completely immerse herself in a bath of clear, cool water, the pool was first filled to a depth of only one inch. Under the watchful eye of her mother on deck, the cub trundled down the stairs and into the water, where she went mad drinking, body splashing, rolling, galloping, and brutally killing floating straw debris. If Bärle had gotten in also, her coat would have sucked up almost all of the water in the pool, leaving little behind for play or experience.

The next day, the pool was filled up to a depth of three inches. Bärle huffed and splashed with her cub in the pool as they batted at and submerged the new buoyant PVC toys and a blue ball, which, at twelve inches in diameter, was only slightly smaller than the cub. When the water level hit four inches, Bärle began what appeared to be the first of many swim lessons, grabbing the cub with her mouth and gently dragging her into the water accompanied by many expressive soft vocals.

In early April, the staff began to acclimate Bärle and her cub to going out onto the tundra by opening the side door of the building next to the transfer. Going about her usual play business, the cub didn't seem to notice, but Bärle did! She was delighted, deeply inhaling the wind-borne information through her nostrils and exhaling spent air through her mouth. When the keepers gave them small piles of tundra dirt and grass, the cub stuck her nose into the pile and breathed in, came out snorting and coughing, and then did it again. She mouth-tested the soil and the grassy clumps and, abandoning all caution, threw herself into the pile and rocked and rolled and wiggled. When she righted herself, she came up looking a lot like Adak during an introduction, covered from head to tail in dirt.

When Bärle began demonstration walking by door nine, we knew she was ready to take her cub outside. Early in the morning on April 13, Bärle ushered her thirty-five-pound, five-month-old cub outside for the first time. For safety, the thirty-thousand-gallon freshwater pool was drained and the moats were filled with several feet of fluffy straw to catch a tumbling bear cub.

With the cub sticking by her as if tethered, Bärle thoroughly inspected the enclosure. She poignantly huffed at the other bears, who were watching the duo from the pack ice. It was impossible

to know if she was greeting them after her lengthy absence, intro-
ducing her new cub, or warning them to stay clear of her cub. Since
Bärle's cub-rearing techniques had thus far been textbook wild
bear behavior, it's likely that Bärle was admonishing her less than
genteel cohorts to stay clear of her baby.

Each day the pool was filled to a slightly deeper level to allow
the cub to get accustomed to it. Bärle had taught her to dog-pad-
dle in the pool room, and in wild play she often dunked her head
under water for a few seconds. Clearly she was not at all comfortable with being underwater; this would take time and experience.

I sat on top of the artificial cliff overlooking the freshwater
pool in the tundra enclosure, inconspicuously making behavior
notes and filming Bärle and her cub. Bärle had greeted me with
an upward head nod, as if smelling the air, and then ignored me.
It was mid-August, four months after their introduction to the
tundra. Over the summer the cub had been named Talini. Now
at almost ten months old, she had grown appreciably and was
roughly the size of an adult midsize dog. She was at that gawky
stage of development—her ears stuck out, giving her a Yoda-like
look, and she had Bigfoot-size paws and the Roman nose of a bull
terrier. On this morning, like every other day, Bärle and Talini were
caught up in water-wrestling.

Talini's latest *modus operandi* was to sneak-attack Bärle by
jumping on her back from shore, resulting in a mutual wrestling hug and roll underwater. On resurfacing, Talini had taken to
play-biting Bärle's jowls and other parts of her face, which had to
hurt even if you were a polar bear. In what appeared to be a teaching session, Bärle gently mouth-grabbed a chunk of fur and skin
on the back of Talini's head and dragged her a few inches into the
water. Wildly aquabatic, Talini flipped over backward, forcing Bärle
to let go. Talini flashed a quick pointy upper lip at her mother;
purposely paw-slammed the surface, shooting water in Bärle's

direction; and retreated to the safety of shore. Her ears were back and she was hanging her head as she got out, and she quickly took a sideways glance up at me. I wondered if she was checking to see if I had witnessed her being chastised by her mother.

Shortly after that came another lesson. Even I had noticed that when the water activities got a little too turbulent, Talini would swim to shore. I recall doing this when I was a child learning to swim. The side of the pool was a safe zone; I could always crawl onto land if I felt further threatened. As I grew more experienced and adept at water sports, I would compose myself while still in the deep end, much as Bärle did. This was a necessary tool when I learned to scuba dive, where swimming to shore or even surfacing is not an option. I imagined it wouldn't be an option for most adult polar bears either.

As she had done the previous dozen times I had just witnessed, Talini dove into the pool behind her mother's back. Hearing the splash, Bärle turned to face off the little shark who was attacking from below. Bärle gently intercepted her and with one paw held her under water slightly longer than before. Talini surfaced and took a breath, and the two embraced in a second roll and wrestled under water. Again Bärle held her under for what seemed to be longer than before. Talini must have detected the difference too, because she first headed for a large floating toy to grab onto. But seeing that Bärle was following her, she swam for shore, this time underwater.

When Bärle was teaching, her expression changed from smiling and open-mouthed laughing to a serious, straight-lined mouth with her eyes and attention fixed on the lesson.

There was only so much teaching that Bärle could do about deep-water swimming in a relatively shallow pool. A few days later, Bärle and Talini were given access to the saltwater pool in the pack ice enclosure. Bärle had a plan. She headed straight for the pool with Talini dawdling along behind her. For every step that Bärle took, Talini took ten, weaving in and out, sniffing this and over-turning that, barely able to keep pace with her mother. Repeatedly Bärle stopped, huffed softly for the cub, and patiently waited for her. When they reached the pool, Bärle walked right into the water, submerged herself, and swam out a short distance. She turned and called to Talini, whose inquisitive activity had come to a grind-ing halt at the water's edge, as if she had just come to the edge of the earth. Bärle persisted, calmly huffing, lightly paw-smacking the surface, coaxing Talini into the water. After feigning interest in pebbles, twigs, bits of straw, and gull feces, Talini stepped belly deep into the pool, then a little farther, then slid and fumbled on all fours back to shore. But she had made a discovery—the water was different, salty. She drank some and promptly vomited.

By Talini's first birthday, in late November, she had become an adept swimmer, wildly porpoising around her mother and engaging her in endless wrestling matches above and below the surface. She had also become more interested in other living things. Humans proved to be excellent interactive fun. Toddlers and babies pressed up against the clear acrylic tunnel walls—sometimes unwillingly by eager parents—were of particular interest. These flailing, often-screeching youngsters, dramatically throwing arms and legs about like whirligigs, captured Talini's attention, and not in good way. She frequently parked her front paws against the underwater window and attempted to press her nose and often-open mouth through the acrylic hoping to engulf a tiny human body part or two. Predictably, the children's reactions were mixed, but the parents seemed oddly entertained by this situation.

I have wondered about this funky human behavior of thrusting helpless loved ones in front of obvious killers to gauge response. The old-style polar bear enclosure at the Calgary Zoo had an observation deck on the roof where visitors could view the bears from above. On a daily basis, zoo visitors would prop their children up onto the railing with their heads, arms, and legs dangling over the pit of these large carnivores, who were intently looking up at them. When I calmly approached the family so as not to startle the parent, whose strong hold on the child was the only thing standing in the way of impending disaster, and asked them to please remove their offspring, I invariably received the same response: "Why, will the polar bears kill my kid?" The fact that the thirty-foot drop into the pit onto a cement floor would likely beat the bears to the punch seemed to escape their notice.

Talini began to recognize individual docents who routinely arrived at the Arctic Ring of Life on weekends to educate the public about polar bears and to dote on Talini in the absence of the public. She tore after Tom Roy, who ran up and down the expansive window in the Exploration Station dangling and swinging lens cases, jackets, and any other handy item in front of him as the chase ensued. One day Carol Bresnay, also a senior docent, brought a dark umbrella with a myriad of brightly colored giraffe designs on it that caught the cub's attention. Mesmerized, Talini pawed gently at the window as Bresnay twirled the open umbrella, displaying a kaleidoscope of color. Bresnay tried the same game with a plain black umbrella, but that did not hold Talini's interest. Talini had noticed, however, that Bresnay would dig deep into her giant purse, which was on the floor in front of the window, to bring out other cub toys, and she would hang upside down in the water with her nose pressed against the window to see what else was in the purse. Then she would visually inspect each item that Bresnay brought out to show her.

Sometimes Talini brought her own things over to the docents. One day she arrived with an arsenal of objects, wearing her toy

O-ring on her forearm like a bracelet while carrying her favorite ball between her front paws. Talini found other ways to have fun as well. Docents were focused on public education when zoo visitors filled the Exploration Station. Standing to the side of the viewing bay with her back to the window, Bresnay would answer questions and explain behaviors. Talini would then covertly dive off the island in the middle of the pool, swim underwater over to the window hugging the pool floor, and suddenly shoot up by the window, popping her head up right next to Bresnay, often smiling or open-mouthed laughing. Caught off guard, zoo visitors were delighted.

Talini frequently incited a riot by vigorously drumming the surface of the water with both paws, causing tidal waves of water to drench the window. Squealing children would race up and down the window between adults' legs, vying for the cub's attention and begging her to play with them. It would be some time before the adults could restore decorum, round up their youngsters, and get them out of the Exploration Station.

Bärle allowed all of this, though she was never far off, carefully monitoring the proceedings. Occasionally she joined in the fun, but often she watched from a distance, looking like a sphinx perched on deck. It seemed to be a welcome reprieve to have babysitters entertaining her cub.

Mothers of singleton cubs have to work double time, since they are both mother and playmate. I was once pressed into nanny duties by Teykova, a Siberian tigress whose recovery from abuse I had assisted in. Teykova was now raising a male cub who was in the tiger equivalent of the terrible twos. Each afternoon I would give her a lovely meaty bone inside the building where it was cool and away from the public. One day when Teykova lay down to enjoy her bone, the cub began to drag the giant bone away from her. Teykova got up, picked up the bone, turned her rear end to the cub, lay down, and resumed eating. Again, the cub ran around to his mother's head and dragged the bone away from her. Teykova got up, picked up the bone, turn her rear end to the cub, lay down, and resumed work on the bone. For the third time, the cub ran around to his mother's head and dragged the bone off. This time Teykova got up, picked up the cub by the scruff of his neck, dropped him off in front of my face where I was crouched down by the fence, and looked me sternly in the eye. Then she walked over to the bone with her rear end toward us, lay down, sighed heavily, and proceeded to work on her bone. I'm not sure who was more surprised—the cub or me. Realizing that I had just been trustingly deputized as a surrogate, I understood that I had better not disappoint her. I stuck the finger of my leather glove through the mesh, and the cub instantly latched onto it for a game of tug-of-war.

Bresnay and the other weekend docents noticed a distinct pattern of behavior emerge. Although Talini was allowed to spend Saturday mornings in rowdy play with the public, the quieter Sunday mornings were devoted to serious teaching sessions. Talini spent those mornings trailing behind Bärle and watching her every move. It was as if Bresnay, other humans, dangling lens cases, jackets, and chromatic umbrellas did not exist; they were simply ignored.

Talini was a substantial-sized bear cub of over one hundred pounds when Bärle began seal-hunting lessons in earnest. What characterized teaching sessions was not only the bears' change in demeanor but the fact that they stayed in the pack ice pool in the vicinity of the giant acrylic windows separating the seals from the polar bears, and the continued repetition of the same hunting techniques practiced over and over again. Three unique hunting strategies were taught, involving stealth, planning, and practice, practice, practice.

Since wild polar bears generally hunt seals by surprising them
when they are hauled out onto the pack ice, or by lying in wait for
them at a breathing hole, or by crash-and-grabs at subnivean dens,
one of Bärle's methods seems likely to have been taught to her by
her wild mother. Bärle would lead Talini up to the island where
they could survey the movement of the seals in their pool when
they routinely swam past certain windows. As a seal approached
a window, Bärle gauged the timing of her flash dive into the pool
and subsequent crash into the submarine window to meet the seal
precisely when he came closest to it. Talini dove after her time and
again to study the assault tactic.

The seals had mixed reactions. The male harbor and harp
seals were visually impaired and showed no signs of knowing or
caring about the bears' intents. Freida, the sighted female harbor
seal, maintained her composure and showed no signs of caring
either way. But Kiinaq, Triton's buddy, the large, young male gray
seal loved the action and took full advantage of this resurgence in
good fortune. He missed Triton and had searched for him through
the windows for weeks after Triton had left for the Indianapolis
Zoo. Kiinaq tried to insinuate himself into the hunt as an intended
victim by hanging out at windows and flapping his fins against
windows where Bärle and Talini were stationed. Bärle's two other
hunting strategies involved hiding behind any of the underwater pillars separating the acrylic windows and lunging at a seal
when he came close to the window. The lunge frequently concluded with a powerful paw-slam against the pane. The extended
version of the lunge-and-paw-slap method included stalking the
seals' movements by swimming on the pool bottom, hiding behind
outcroppings, and blending in with the scenery by remaining completely motionless if caught out in the open.

Talini swam steadfastly in tandem behind her mother. She was
a quick study, and within weeks was practicing hunting techniques

on her own. With a significant amount of classroom disturbance and interference from Kiinaq, Talini ended up developing a close play relationship with him, just as her father had.

Talini had her own rendition of Bärle's hunting technique. Carrie McIntyre, a senior docent who also worked weekends, repeatedly observed Talini lying motionless on top of the water, watching, waiting, and seemingly not moving a muscle. When an unsuspecting seal approached a window, this mock ice floe hideously sprang to life and pounced at the prey. This was Talini's preferred hunting strategy and she carried it on into her adult life.

By her second birthday, in late November 2006, Talini had grown to well over two hundred pounds. The period of natural dispersion, when Bärle would convince Talini that they needed to part ways, would be upon them in the spring.

In anticipation of this time, Adak had been introduced to Bärle and Talini so that the cub could learn to live peaceably with other bears in the group. Bärle's closest female companion, Vilma, would have been the obvious first choice to rebuild a group around mother and cub, but, sadly, Vilma had died in June at the age of twenty-four. Politically astute Icee would have been a good choice too, but she too had died at the age of twenty-four, in May 2005, one year after Triton left. Although there is no doubt that Bärle understood that Vilma and Icee were gone, she was completely absorbed in the job of raising Talini and her behaviors remained unchanged. Her parental duties were not yet complete, and she was still very protective of her offspring, which was good, because Adak needed some bossing around.

To help celebrate Talini's second birthday, the keepers made a giant barrel-sized three-layer ice cake infused with peanut butter, honey, Jell-O, bagels, polar bear chow, and, of course, fish. And they made a smaller, more utilitarian frozen treat containing fish,

apples, and pears. Talini arrived at the large ice cake first, followed
by Bärle, who had stood back a few minutes to allow Talini first
choice. Adak feigned interest in the lesser ice treat some distance   181
away but frequently took peripheral glances at the others. Cautiously, he attempted to sidle up to the couple but stopped within
ten feet of the celebration. Adak leaned forward as if to circle them,
asking for permission to eat with them, but Bärle did not acknowledge his presence and the answer must have been no, because he
left. It's possible that Bärle was allowing Talini to make the decision, since customarily the first bears at the cache seem to control
access. Later Adak found that the celebration cake had been broken into two pieces that were at least ten feet apart. Bärle was
eating one piece, so he cautiously approached the second piece
and began eating it. Immediately, Bärle hustled over to him and
bellowed in his face. Ignoring her, Adak calmly kept eating, standing his ground. Talini rushed over and took possession of the first
piece. Bärle settled on this arrangement and joined Talini.

Over the winter, Bärle grew progressively more comfortable
with Adak's behavior toward Talini, admonishing him less as
Talini learned to negotiate for herself. She had the typical attitude
that every well-raised singleton bear cub has. She thought the
world revolved around her and her well-being, an attitude that
presumably is eventually knocked out of such cubs by siblings, by
other subadults and adults after dispersal, or by the circumstances
of survival.

Well, that didn't happen here. It turned out that Adak was completely enamored of this young, energetic, playful little female,
and he indulged her whims almost as much as her mother did.
They played for endless hours together, wrestling in the pool.
Adak wrapped his forearms around her waist as if in a breeding
stance. Talini, who had not yet reached sexual maturity, did not

understand the significance of this and enthusiastically wrestled her way out of these strongholds again and again. Although their play behavior resembled breeding activity, there was a line that Adak never crossed. He did not attempt to copulate with her; nor did he court her. They simply wrestled in the pool, on land, in the building, whenever and wherever the mood struck them. He was gentle and considerate, and this twenty-eight-year-old, sometimes socially clumsy male bear earned a new nickname, Uncle Adak. This phenomenon has been observed before in captivity that old male bears can be very tolerant and enjoy playing with younger animals.

As the snow melted and ushered in new spring growth in 2007, Bärle was changing too. She separated herself from Talini and became preoccupied with Norton, across the moat. She was abrupt with Talini and chased her away from food and nests. Bärle didn't want to play or cuddle with her, and worst of all, Bärle didn't want to nest together anymore.

Talini was devastated, and sometimes regressed into a clingy, whiny cublet. Adak noticed the change in Bärle before the humans did and began to court her. Far from being the center of everyone's universe, Talini now found that she was in the way. Things were happening around her that she did not understand, and in the crowd of bears she was alone. On occasion, Adak came back to check on her reproductive status by sniffing and sidling up to her, a normal male behavior, which she did not understand, but eventually he returned to being playful Uncle Adak. There were always docents to play with on the weekend and seals and children to hunt, but it was not the same.

Bärle and Norton were reintroduced for breeding season, leaving Adak and Talini to watch from across the moat. For days Talini bawled and called for her mother's attention. But Bärle was busy, focused entirely on the dance of courtship with her attentive suitor. She ate with Norton, traveled with him, and slept with him—all of the things she used to do with Talini. But Bärle's duties as a mother were only complete in this final teaching session. Watching, Talini was learning a critical skill that could save her life and the species. Talini was learning how to maneuver with those enormous breeding males. As time passed, Adak's and Talini's attention turned back toward each other. Talini was not cycling, so there was only one thing left for them to do—play, play, and play some more.

On Talini's third birthday, Betsie Meister made her another giant three-layer ice cake full of fabulous treats that Talini shared with Adak. Adak got there first and licked and gnawed at the honey on one side. When he went down to the pool to have a drink, Talini arrived and began work on the opposite side. Adak returned and recommenced work on his side, but he was not happy. Talini was using her claw to scrape bagel shavings off the cake then licking them up. Adak stopped licking and open-mouthed mock-bit her upper jaw, telling her that she should stop. Talini ignored him and continued to scrape and lick. She had a small self-assured smile on her face. Adak persisted and gently mock-bit her paw to make her stop. Talini continued for a few more seconds, then calmly changed position and began work on another part of the cake. She had learned. She was wisely negotiating with other bears.

Seasons came and went, as did males for both Bärle and Talini. Although Bärle skillfully bred with other males, and denned up in the winter in her apartment, she never again gave birth to a cub. She was getting old and was slowing down. It's possible that over-wintering in a den full of soft, fresh straw, with room-service meals, offered her a warm reprieve from the cold in her old age. "What Bärle wants, Bärle gets."

In July 2012, Bärle lost her appetite. Keepers tried all of her favorites. Cans of tuna and salmon were opened. A myriad of fish species materialized. Peanut butter was spread on a dozen different types of bread. Fruits and vegetables were sliced, diced, smashed, and cooked. Nothing worked. Yams were cooked and chickens roasted. Handfuls of savory meat were ripped off and offered through the mesh. Again, nothing worked.

On the morning of July 18, Bärle was knocked down for a veterinary checkup, and the veterinarian discovered tumors throughout her abdominal cavity. She was euthanized at the age of twenty-eight. Afterward the building felt strangely empty; staff members were strangely silent. The battle for survival for this regal, determined polar bear was finally over.

It was later determined in the necropsy that among other things, Bärle had liver cancer and her lymph nodes were abnormal and enlarged. Bärle had arrived at the Detroit Zoo a living hull with a grip on life that would not let go. True to bear character, she took full advantage of improvements offered to her that allowed her to express herself without consequence. She transformed herself from a circus act to a polar bear, undoing some of the harm that her entanglement with human greed had caused her.

10

DOES ONE BEAR'S LIFE MATTER?

Asking Questions

BÄRLE WOULD NOT have been rescued had it not been for the questions Ken and Sherri Gigliotti asked in Cozumel, Mexico, in 1996. After thirteen years of marriage, the couple had decided it was high time they had a honeymoon trip. Living in Winnipeg, Manitoba, frequently said to be the land of wind, ice, and snow, they did what Canadians traditionally do on vacation—they traveled south to Mexico. In an orientation session given on their arrival at the hotel in Cozumel, the tour guide told them that the Canadians in the group would be interested to know that a circus featuring polar bears was coming to town in a few days. Ken and Sherri couldn't believe it. Polar bears, in a circus, in Mexico? How could that even be possible? Several days later, Sherri was surprised to see a circus across the street from their hotel in Cozumel that had mushroomed out of the ground overnight.

That morning they investigated the setup and tried to get tickets for that night's performance. It was like stepping back in time. There was a high-top tent, and seven polar bears were held in tiny barred wagons. They were dirty, hot, and suffering. Sherri noted, "If they had even a cup of water, then that was stretching it."[1] The

Gigliottis knew they had to be careful. Ken, an award-winning photojournalist at the *Winnipeg Free Press,* had not taken a camera with him, because he didn't want to arouse suspicion. But something seemed to have given away their disapproval.

That evening, when they were seated in the front row for the performance, they were told that no one was allowed to take photographs. No programs—which were full of photographs of the bears and their hideous circumstances—were being sold either. Determined to bring some evidence of the bears' suffering back to Canada, Sherri approached numerous circus staff and begged for a copy of the pamphlet. "Oh, please, may I have one?" she said. "It would mean so much to me to be able to have this program as a memento of our vacation." An employee relented and secretly gave her one. That one act changed these bears' lives.

On their return to Winnipeg, the *Winnipeg Free Press* published their story and some of the program photographs, which outraged the international community. In a personal communication, I asked the Gigliottis why they had done something about the bears' situation when thousands of others, some media professionals, had not. They responded:

It is everyone's fundamental responsibility to advocate for those who cannot. Once you see or become aware of abuse, if you walk away or turn your head you become equally responsible for the continued abuse to occur. Anything you do [to help] leads to a progressive stop of the abuse and the beginning of a healing process. It does not have to be anything heroic. We were told that some of the bears came from Churchill, Manitoba, and we are from Winnipeg. That made it personal to us and we were upset, shocked, and appalled that these magnificent animals could be so out of place and so far from home.

Is it dignified or respectful for humans to acquire wild animals for entertainment purposes?

We came back from our honeymoon with a circus program
and a story with a local connection. This created a ripple effect
that resulted in the eventual rescue of these majestic polar bears
from a life of daily abuse in deplorable conditions. We understand that most of the bears have now passed on but that their
final days were not spent performing in a small traveling circus
too far from home. Thanks to so many people, at so many levels,
in so many countries, who gave these bears a second chance, and
ultimately made such a difference.[2]

Does one bear's life matter? This is a simple question with a
simple answer: Yes, it matters to that bear. There shouldn't even
be a debate on the subject, since generation after generation of
humans have watched individual captive and wild bears make
extraordinary attempts to adapt in order to survive. Charles Darwin is frequently misquoted as having said, "In the struggle for
survival, the fittest win out at the expense of their rivals because
they succeed in adapting themselves best to their environment."
This quote is rightly attributed to Leon C. Megginson, a marketing
professor at Louisiana State University, who was trying to encap-
sulate Darwin's essence of evolution. Darwin, however, focused not
on the survival of an individual but on the survival of a species
because of the plasticity of its genetic material. A strong genetic
urge to preserve one's own self makes the wheels of evolution turn.

Bärle is a prime example of the struggle to survive by attempting to adapt to a hostile environment, as she tried again and again
to retrofit her polar bear traits to the inhospitable human world of
circus life. When a bear is forced to do this, his ability to compro-
mise is stretched beyond capacity until, sometimes, it snaps. And

yet humans who are foolish enough to go in with the bears they dominate are occasionally injured or killed. Since 2008, there has been at least one death or injury per year of trainers or bystanders by captive bears. The mystery is not why it happens this often; the mystery is why it does not happen more often. The answer lies in the complicated psychological mash of learned helplessness, terror, and the bears' ability to make risk-management decisions ensuring, above all else, their own survival.

I asked several bear experts if the life of one bear matters. Debbie Leahy, who spent hundreds of hours advocating for Bärle and her companions' rescue, responded:

> If we have an opportunity to eliminate suffering, we must try, whether it's for one animal or many. The rescue of a single bear from deprived and abusive conditions helps not only that bear, but other bears and other animals in similar situations through the awareness generated about the plight of that animal. People connect more with an issue if they get to know and understand an individual animal and can follow that animal's transformation from a life of misery to one where they receive the best possible care that captivity has to offer. The many people who followed Bärle's story now have a better understanding of how difficult captivity can be for bears and how all animals in circuses suffer through the most horrendous conditions. There are perhaps thousands of bears going mad in flimsy backyard cages and cramped, barren cages in roadside zoos and traveling circuses. With inspirational stories like Bärle's, more people come to understand that such a deprived life is unacceptable and will support efforts to make substantial changes, such as much stronger laws and better enforcement of existing laws. And, equally important, they will choose not to patronize outdated

attractions that subject these highly intelligent, curious, energetic, and long-lived animals to such gross mistreatment.[3]

Sarah Bexell, author of *Giant Pandas: Born Survivors,* has spent
fifteen years working in the field of conservation education in
the United States and China. I asked her that same question, and
she said:

> Does one bear's life matter!? Of course... Every bear wants to
> live, to thrive, to explore the world, to live out their life as a bear
> should; with beauty and wonder and delicious berries, honey, or
> fish all around (or if a panda, bamboo literally all around!), with
> precious cubs to raise and protect and teach to climb and find
> food, to court and to mate and to sleep in peace. The life of every
> bear matters, to them, to me, and to any human who still has a
> brain and a heart.[4]

It's difficult to argue against the fact that a bear has a right to live
in captivity without abuse or has a right to exist at all. Perhaps the
question is not "Does one bear's life matter?" Perhaps the more
adroit question is "When does a bear's life matter?" A disconnect
occurs when the bear's agenda conflicts with the human agenda,
and the human agenda is most often based on money. Bears never
thrive when cared for strictly within the confines of the human
agenda. The most recent globally sensational example of a bear's
life that was squashed by anthropocentrism was the tragic life of
Knut, the polar bear from the Berlin Zoo.

On November 27, 2005, a twenty-year-old captive female
polar bear named Tosca gave birth to three male cubs at the Berlin Zoological Garden, in Berlin's Großer Tiergarten. Two cubs
died that day, and the surviving cub died one week later. It is not

known if the remaining neonate was rescued by staff and hand-raising attempts failed. Tosca was immediately bred again and gave birth to twin male cubs on December 5, 2006. Three days after the birth, the keepers found the cubs abandoned by their mother on the cement rocks in the outdoor enclosure. The zookeepers rescued the tiny bears by fishing them out of the enclosure with a dip net. One cub reportedly died of pneumonia, but a male cub later named Knut survived. A wild public debate ensued in the media as to whether or not Knut should be allowed to live.

Frank Albrecht of PETA was quoted as saying, "If truth be told, the zoo should have killed the baby bear."[5] Wolfram Graf-Rudolf, director of the Aachen Zoo, apparently agreed, saying, "One should have the courage to let the bear die."[6] This was fodder for journalists who had little understanding of the needs of captive bears but knew how to appeal to human emotion to sell the news.

International news agencies grabbed hold of the story, kindergarten children marched on the Berlin Zoo carrying placards spell-checked by doting parents, people on both sides of the issue threatened bodily harm to those on the other side, and self-aggrandizing emotional statements steeped in entitlement thinking were tweeted, Facebooked, and blogged, saturating social media. Andre Schuele, the Berlin Zoo veterinarian, defended the zoo's decision, arguing that each circumstance must be assessed on its own merits and that "Knut was a healthy baby bear when we found him and so there was no reason for us to put him down."[7]

This frenzied debate came after the fact. The appropriate question was not "Should Knut have been allowed to live?" The appropriate question was "Should Knut have been born?" Knut's mother, Tosca, is another polar bear with an obscure history, shrouded in clandestine dealings and mysterious paperwork. She is recorded in the 2010 *International Studbook for Polar Bears* produced by the World Association of Zoos and Aquariums as having been born in the wild circa 1986, and then, like Kenny and Boris, she appeared in the State Circus of the German Repub- lic in 1987, working with Ursula Böttcher. Böttcher tells adoring fans that Tosca is Kenny's sister and that they are Canadian bears. Since the discovery that Kenny did not have the Government of Manitoba tattoo, however, his legal Canadian status, at least, is in question. Other sources within the zoo community speculate that Tosca most likely came from the wilds of Soviet Russia, in which case it's possible that Kenny did too. In the world of circus subterfuge, all things are possible, including the prospect that the bears known as Tosca and Kenny are not the original bears with those names at all. Tosca was moved to the Berlin Zoo in 1998, when the circus dissolved and Böttcher retired.

Tosca's history suggests an obvious inability to raise young. If the records are accurate, then Tosca, like Bärle, spent approximately a dozen years suffering in the circus world. It is unlikely that Tosca was offered an intensive recovery program, as Bärle was, on her arrival at the Berlin Zoo, since at that time trauma was not recognized in animals and recovery programs for animals did not exist. One fact remains certain: Tosca has never successfully raised a bear cub. This failure could be a result of her traumatic circus history as well as the constant stress of her current living conditions. Walking through the gates at the Berlin Zoo in 2012 was for me like stepping back in time fifty years. The zoo's barren cement enclosures were vestiges of an age gone by when zoos acquired animal species as if they were Noah filling an ark. The construction of the polar bear exhibit that Tosca and her cagemates live in today was completed in 1969. It was designed with the traditional features of that era, including tiny back rooms no bigger than eighty square feet, with everything constructed exclusively of cement and rock.

An astonishing 2,600 tons of granite was imported from Bavaria and shipped over 250 miles to Berlin to build this sepulchre.

Today we know that these impoverished cement and rock, sensory-depriving pits cause serious mental and physical problems for bears and other species. Responsible zoos that cannot afford to immediately construct new natural enclosures spend lesser sums of money to upgrade by adding natural substrates, species-specific environmental enrichment programming, appropriate furniture like climbing structures and bedding material, and seasonally appropriate behavior-based husbandry routines such as changes in diet.

The Berlin Zoo has done none of these things, and as a result many of its animals, including bears, languish in bleak, stagnant exhibits. It was unnerving, a bit like touring a cemetery full of memorial mausoleums, with one horrific exception—these sarcophagi contained live animals rhythmically pacing back and forth. I took a video of Tosca on a small island, deeply entrenched in her daily pacing pattern, two steps forward, and four smaller steps backward while swinging her head mechanically from side to side. This pattern persisted for several hours. I have been told by locals that she paces like this for much of the day and has done so since she arrived from the circus twenty-three years ago. I did the math. Between December of 2006 and March of 2011, Tosca had been dancing her swan song for approximately twelve million Knut fans, to say nothing of the millions of visitors she has entertained in her circus years and before and after Knut's short life.

Incredibly, after five unsuccessful attempts at nurturing cubs within a twelve-month period, the zoo bred Tosca again in 2008 without making any attempts to mitigate her trauma. On December 18 of that year, she gave birth to two male cubs, who, predictably, died on December 21 because of lack of maternal care. A popular quote sometimes attributed to Albert Einstein defines insanity as repeating the same behavior over and over again without interjecting anything new into the mix and expecting a different outcome. The Berlin Zoo's managerial behavior leads one to ask what the heck they were thinking. Societal impetus in Berlin has allowed management not to keep up with modern husbandry methods that allow wildlife to thrive. The zoo has even described itself as a living museum paying homage to historical zookeeping.

Zoos are definitely a product of their social environment. I like Berlin. It is the most interesting and complex city I have had the good fortune to work in. Berlin is a city of extreme dichotomies where old and new thinking coexist like oil and water in a spinning blender. It is dotted with both uber-modern and historical architecture, as well as monuments to some of the world's most grievous atrocities, never to be forgotten, and according to the younger generation, never to be repeated. I was thoroughly impressed with the local young people I met there who are burdened with the monstrous responsibility of cleaning up the mess their parents and grandparents have left them. In Berlin, the war is not over, and a younger generation, who had nothing to do with any of it, lives with its aftermath every day. When the Berlin Wall came down in 1989, the life-altering challenge of the reunification of East and West Berlin and its families came with the unenviable task of healing not just from history's human carnage but from broken ideologies that are still extant today. It is in this arena of human recovery from generations of trauma that animals at the zoo are still allowed to languish behind walls and in cages. But the waves of reunification and inevitable modernization are lapping at the heels of zoo management, and there is no doubt that soon there will be a tidal wave of change.

Updating the zoo will be both costly and time-consuming. It will involve consultation with international zoo professionals, staff training, public education, and an extensive plan to assess the recovery needs of each animal. The good news is that Tosca and the other animals in the zoo do not have to wait until natural enclosures can be built. If modern husbandry techniques are implemented, the bears could benefit immediately from an intelligent, measured infusion of species-specific enrichment. Like Bärle, Tosca will need time to acclimate to greater and greater complexity in a step-by-step approach to bring her back to life. A recovery plan needs to be developed for her that specifically addresses her current aberrant behaviors. In the interim, zookeepers can begin the process simply by making straw available to Tosca and her companions for nest building. It is one of the least expensive and simplest forms of enrichment, and it is greatly appreciated by traumatized bears. Upon her arrival at the Detroit Zoo, Bärle honed in on her pile of fresh, clean straw like a missile. Tosca will do the same. One of the most common refrains from old-school managers, who also need to be acclimated to complexity in husbandry, is that the straw will clog their ancient drains. This problem could easily be resolved by using grates over drains, water rakes, and some ingenuity.

For every new idea presented there will be naysayers. Some of the common roadblocks to increasing the complexity of the polar bears' environment are the requirement that the enrichment be all-natural so that the exhibit looks like the Arctic; the argument that the zoo does not have the staff to make and clean up enrichment; and the belief that objects in the exhibit may hurt the bear. To inspired thinkers, the solutions are relatively simple, and whatever problems are encountered should not be used as an excuse not to make improvements. In no way does a solid cement exhibit appear to resemble the Arctic, subarctic, or any other natural environment on this planet. Therefore, until a natural habitat can replace the cement and rock fortress, enrichment must focus on the bear's recovery needs. Incorporating enrichment into the daily husbandry plan is labor-intensive, but zoos with small budgets and staff shortages can develop volunteer programs to help. Volunteers can be taught to construct enrichment items, and others can act as animal care aides, working alongside a zookeeper during cleanup. Enrichment objects must be safe for bears to use within reason. For safety, old-school thinking from the 1950s promoted completely barren environments devoid of any objects other than food. Ironically, as a result, sensory-deprived creatures struggling to express their genetic urges handled feces, pulled out their fur and feathers, and developed deeply entrenched repetitive behaviors.

Knut's life was a byproduct of Tosca's as-yet-unabated suffering. After the controversy over his death, the fervor died, only to reignite when his hide was tanned, stretched over a polyurethane body, and put on display at the Berlin Museum of Natural Science as an attraction acting more as a memorial to the human agenda than an educational tool. Meanwhile, Tosca is still pacing at the Berlin Zoo. Here is an opportunity for the millions of adoring Knut fans, the journalists, the politicians, the zoo community, the animal activist groups, and those passionate about polar bear welfare to roll up their sleeves, get to work, and make a real difference by asking questions and advocating for her welfare. Will change come soon enough for Tosca and her companions to realize the same joy that Bärle expressed when she unabashedly threw herself into a clean bale of straw for the first time and rubbed, rocked, and rolled? A movement to help Tosca will require everyone to change tracks from the self-interest of the human agenda to Tosca's agenda.

Focused exclusively on the animal agenda, Jill Robinson has spent a lifetime working in Asia to rescue bears. She is utterly unconcerned about the human agenda. In 1993, she exposed the world to the cruel practice of bear bile farming in China, and in 1998, founded Animals Asia, which has grown to be an internationally respected nonprofit organization whose mission is to end bear bile farming and the cruel and illegal trade in dogs and cats for human consumption as well as to improve the respect and welfare of animals in zoos. Animals Asia operates two bear sanctuaries, in China and Vietnam, and has rescued and recovered well over four hundred bears. Thousands of bears still languish in farms in Asia, however.

Robinson's unwavering dedication to the animal agenda has garnered the respect and awe of thousands of people worldwide, who have showered her with well-deserved human honors. She has received an honorary doctorate from the University of Zurich and is an Asia World Animal Day ambassador, a council member of the World Federation of Chinese Medicine Societies Herbal Committee, a British Broadcasting Company Wildlife Magazine Conservation hero, and a member of the U.S. Society of Women Geographers. In 1998, Robinson was awarded Member of the Order of the British Empire by Queen Elizabeth.

I have spent time in Robinson's company, and I get the impression that although she is humbled and somewhat embarrassed by the human accolades, the smile on a recovered bear's face means more to her than if Queen Elizabeth herself had handed Robinson the crown jewels.

In a personal communication, I asked her whether one bear's life matters. With her characteristically high regard for the animals' agenda, Robinson responded:

Every bear who steps through our sanctuary doors in China and Vietnam shows, in his or her own way, their right to life—and why that life, their only life, matters. We have seen some terrible things. Bears arriving skeletally thin and literally shells of the animals they would be in the wild. Liver cancers up to

15.5 pounds in weight, and limbs that are missing from the ravages of snares, or that have been self-mutilated as a result of their years of stress and pain on the farms. Sick to our stomachs we have euthanized them immediately when we have realized that there is literally nothing we can do—and mourn for the lives they lost at the hands of farmers who greedily exploited them all.

Jasper's cage was a rusting prison of torture. This miserable creature's body had been pressed against the bars by a "crush" which had reduced the height of the cage by half and flattened his frame to the floor. Unable to sit or stand, or barely move, and with a dirty metal catheter crudely embedded into his abdomen and gall bladder, this sensitive, intelligent bear lay there on one of China's notorious bear farms for fifteen years of his life. [8]

She explains further:

Over ten thousand bears (mainly moon bears, but brown and sun bears too) are incarcerated on farms across Asia, and cruelly milked for their bile, despite the availability of herbal and synthetic alternatives. Generally every bear that has suffered bile extraction requires radical surgery and other medical procedures to "mend" their broken bodies. Diseased gall bladders are routinely removed; smashed and rotting teeth are repaired or removed too, while bears suffering from eye, arthritis, or heart problems are treated for the rest of their lives. Those clearly suffering from serious cancer or advanced mobility issues are gently euthanized by a team who have given them the only respect they have encountered after years—and even decades—of exploitation on the farms. Animals Asia has rescued over four hundred bears in award-winning sanctuaries in China and Vietnam.

Today, Jasper is called the "peacemaker" of the sanctuary, as he welcomes new arrivals with the friendliness of an old patriarch, and finds time to rough and tumble with the juveniles in what we affectionately call "bear bundles of play." He will even step in to prevent the odd disagreement between other bears, and for a bear crushed flat to the bottom of his cage for fifteen years, we find his charisma and kindness astonishing.

Jasper's life matters to those of us who document the species of Asiatic black bears; their behavior, their physiology, their responses to multiple surgeries and medical procedures, their adaptive behavior in social groups, and their stoic, indomitable characters. Most of all, Jasper's life matters as much to him as it does to the bears with whom he socializes, and it matters to those who hear his story today and feel compelled to help relegate this horrible industry to the history books of shame.

Franzi was rescued just in time. She arrived as an old, sick bear in the tiniest cage we had ever seen, and broke and won our hearts from the start. Franzi had been deliberately declawed and de-toothed, and had a horrible pus-infected wound in her abdomen which was created through surgical mutilation on the farm. Ironically, this "free drip fistula" is the only method of bile extraction officially allowed in China and allowed her to be milked, like a machine, for twenty-two years of her life. More than anything, Franzi's eyes said it all. She would look up from staring at the floor of her recovery cage, gaze sadly into our eyes for a few seconds, before returning her stare to the corner of the cage, retreating into her world of misery and despair.[9]

With the expert care of Robinson and her team, the little dwarf bear Franzi lived an enriched and meaningful life for another seven years in her own quiet "secret garden" together with a brain-damaged male bear named Rupert, who doted on her. Although Franzi initially rebuffed him, she eventually warmed up to Rupert's adoring attention, and the two were often found nuzzled up together in the grass, snoozing in the warm afternoon sun.

Despite lung, heart, and digestion problems as well as other physical handicaps, Franzi learned to trust her caregivers to the point where she felt safe spitting out apple pieces with peel that she could not chew, knowing that she would immediately be presented with peeled apple pieces that could be gummed.

Robinson continued:

> Franzi passed away in October 2009, followed by Rupert about six months later, and the words of Tolstoy could have been written just for them, "Every man and every living creature has the sacred right to the gladness of spring." Franzi's life mattered to her, and to everyone who met her, acknowledging her as a perfect example of an animal that deserved those final few years in the spring, and one showing forgiveness for her past.[10]

Today, Animals Asia has its work cut out for it. China has a history of dealing in wildlife as commodities, as exemplified by their mass production and international rental or sale of panda bears, which Canada has both historically and recently taken part in. On March 25, 2013, Prime Minister Harper greeted a pair of young giant pandas at the Toronto Pearson International Airport, calling them "international treasures."[11] I had hoped that Prime Minister Harper would have considered polar bears to be an international treasure as well. In addition to pandas, China has also perfected the artificial insemination of polar bears, speculating that international trade in that species could be taking off. In December 2012, a tiny male polar bear cub was born to an artificially inseminated female at Tianjin Haichang Polar Ocean World in China. He was then taken away from his mother and hand-raised by human workers. In April 2013, at only four months old, this cub made the arduous flight from China over Europe to British Columbia. He was imported by Beyond Just Bears, a company that trains exotic and domestic animals for entertainment in movies and commercials and on television. According to the Amended Controlled Alien Species Permit issued by the Government of British Columbia, the cub, named Tiger, was to spend thirty days in quarantine in British Columbia, and then be moved to Winnipeg for a commercial filming venture. Ironically, the storyline of the movie *Midnight Sun*, which the cub is starring in, revolves around a boy who risks his life trying to reunite a baby polar bear with his mother in the Arctic. After filming, the cub was sent back to China. The importation of the cub was allowed only because there is no provincial or federal legislation in Canada to protect him.

In March 2013 in Bangkok, the Convention on International Trade in Endangered Species (CITES) Conference of Parties failed to upgrade polar bears from its Appendix II, wherein trade is allowed but controlled, to Appendix I, wherein all trade is suspended. The most commonly cited reason for this failure is that illegal trade in polar bears may increase if upgraded. Considering that the global demand for polar bear pelts has already increased at fur auctions by 375 percent between 2007 and 2012, one could argue that this ship has sailed. The importation of polar bears into the United States is illegal, however, and the species is protected under the United States Marine Mammals Protection Act.

So, what does this little Chinese polar bear cub have to look forward to? A lifetime of learning stunts and tricks for human entertainment and being shunted in a caravan from one location to the next. Beyond Just Bears already owns one polar bear, a seventeen-year-old adult female bear named Agee, from the Kolmården Zoo in Sweden. The life she is living seems to fore-shadow what lies ahead for the Chinese polar bear cub. A YouTube video produced by the *Province* newspaper shows the barren inte-rior of the trailer and the minuscule adjoining pool. In an alarming statement, the trainer says, "And little bears are all the same. They have tempers when they're little. And you know, like a grizzly bear has a temper when he's bigger. He still has that temper. And you know, you just have to teach him to control it."[12] It has been my experience that bears do not have tempers as much as they have the desire for self-determination. When their genetically inherited behavior comes into conflict with the human agenda, as it does when they are trained for entertainment, bears are conflicted and will do what they have to, to express themselves.

Canada has two-thirds of the world's population of polar bears. Why, then, is it importing polar bears from China or Sweden? Canadians must ask themselves if they believe that Canada should become the country of choice for questionable animal welfare practices that have been outlawed in the United States. Individu-als can advocate for the protection of polar bears and other wildlife in a number of different government arenas. Municipalities can ban the private or corporate ownership of exotic animals. When provincial governments pass legislation protecting indigenous animals, they should include those individuals born and raised in captivity and those imported from other countries. The Govern-ment of Canada needs to develop a marine mammals protection act that includes polar bears as well as seal and whale species.

Privately, we all must ask questions of advertising agencies, moviemakers, and television networks. In 2010, Nissan produced a commercial with Agee for its new electric car, the Nissan Leaf. The world of entertainment is every bit as ethereal and culpable as the circus world. Utterly ignoring the plight of animals forced to work in the field of entertainment, Nissan uses emotional sentiment to make money at Agee's expense and promotes its vehicle as nature friendly. Consumers can register their concerns by not patronizing the companies that produce commercials, movies, and television programs off the backs of wildlife forced to work in the industry. When you see a bear in entertainment, ask, "Who is this bear?" and "Why is he in this product?"

Hauser Bears is an international charitable organization committed to the global conservation of bears with a focus on help for bears trapped in the entertainment industry, on the issues of bear bile farming in South East Asia, and on the poaching of wild bears for body parts. The organization's cofounders, sisters Karine and Anna Hauser, are deeply committed to compassion for both captive and wild bears. Often when the world considers the health of bear populations, the interests of one animal are lost in the crowd, and conservation becomes a numbers game. But populations are made up of individuals. When asked, "Does one bear's life matter?" Karine Hauser responded:

> Asking ourselves [that question] can be answered in many different ways. From a conservation viewpoint, we cannot be so arrogant as to think that we know at which point we haven't got enough individuals to keep a species going. We do not know what the future holds and how the many factors that contribute to a thriving population will vary. Destruction will happen no matter what the intentions are, merely due to the size of our population encroaching on precious habitat and depleting resources shared with other species such as bears. But putting aside conservation considerations for a moment, leads to a further question: "Does our value system dictate that compassion

should extend to other species such as bears?" The definition of compassion is "the understanding or empathy for the suffering of others," an emotion which is in effect vital for the survival of our own species. It is a value central to our social structure, which enables us to be more successful. We now have enough of an understanding of the world, to know that our own survival depends on the existence of balanced ecosystems and biodiversity. Going forward, we need other species to survive alongside us, and bears particularly play a very important role in maintaining that healthy biodiversity. To protect these species we must extend our compassion to them. Emotions are the biggest drivers in any decision-making process, regardless of how cerebral we think we are. This incredibly powerful emotion of empathy for the suffering and the demise of an individual from another species should underpin our actions toward protecting them, if they are to be successful.[13]

I and my colleagues—Debbie Leahy, Scott Carter, Diana Weinhardt, Jeff Owen, Tim Mengel, Ann Duncan, Chris Bartos, Holly Reed, Betsie Meister, and hundreds of others—owe Ken and Sherri Gigliotti a debt of gratitude. Their first move, their brave and unselfish yet simple act of indignation, changed the lives of bears and humans alike.

I was completely disarmed that first time I saw those innocent eyes looking at me from a worn face in the crate at the FedEx hangar in Detroit. As time passed and Bärle grew stronger and more experienced, her eyes gradually began to reflect the knowledge she was gaining about herself and healthy polar bear behaviors and interrelationships until finally her whole face shone with the pride and the wisdom of an adult female polar bear successfully raising her cub. Gone was the cub-like innocence that she did not have the chance to outgrow in a circus world completely devoid of meaningful stimuli to a polar bear's genetic sensibilities. Although Bärle arrived as an adult bear, we had the privilege of watching her blossom into a self-reliant, expressive, and capable polar bear.

Scott Carter, chief life sciences officer at the Detroit Zoo commented:

> Bärle's was such a gratifying rescue. She is one of the great rescue stories. I think, so often, humans tend to look at animals that are physically or mentally damaged as if there's no hope; "there's no reason to even do a rescue," "this animal will never be right." Bärle showed us that animals can recover; even animals who have been severely abused for years can recover. Bärle is that example that tells us there is reason to hope.[14]

If we care about bears, we must do more than buy the T-shirt and the stuffed bear and go home. We must ask these two life-giving questions, "Where did this bear come from?" and "Why is she here?" and then do the right thing—focus on the animal's agenda.

So, "Where did Bärle come from?" Her history is murky; her records are steeped in human greed and deceit. But Bärle herself told us that she was a wild bear. She raised a mentally and physically healthy polar bear cub so skillfully that her mother's wild teaching emanated from her behavior. Human-raised bears have a great deal of difficulty raising their own young, since they have little to no personal experience of mothering. Bärle never strayed from her conviction that seals were for eating and seal hunting was serious business. She taught as much to her cub. Talini learned to hunt seals, but like her father, Triton, who was also a first-generation captive bear, she befriended Kiinaq for play. Bärle did not. "Why was Bärle at the Detroit Zoo?" To recover! From the day she stepped out of the crate and into the quarantine room at the Detroit Zoo animal hospital to the day she stepped out of door nine and into the tundra enclosure at the ARL to show off her new cub, Bärle bravely took advantage of every opportunity offered to her to learn, to make mistakes, and to try again to rebuild herself as a polar bear. Her life mattered to her, to the bears she lived with, to me, and to thousands of humans.

NOTES

CHAPTER ONE

1   Debbie Leahy, Captive Wildlife Regulatory Specialist, Humane Society of the United States, personal communication, April 27, 2012.

2   Ibid.

3   Robert Brandis, United States Department of Agriculture (USDA), Animal and Plant Health Inspection Service (APHIS), Animal Care, Inspector ID. 2002, Inspection Report 94-C-0112, August 29, 2001.

4   Adam M. Roberts, "Polar Bears Suffer in the Suarez Brothers Circus," *Animal Welfare Institute Quarterly* 51, no. 1 (2002).

5   Ibid.

6   CBC News, Canadian Broadcasting Company, "Resolute Loses Chinese Polar Bear Hunt—Business Bows to Pressure from International Media Deriding Hunt of 'Endangered' Bears," March 9, 2012. www.cbc.ca/news/canada/north/resolute-loses-chinese-polar-bear-hunt-1.1213878 (accessed April 5, 2014).

7   Peter Simpson, "Chinese Thrill Seekers Paying £50,000 for 'Trip of a Lifetime' ... to Kill Endangered Polar Bears," Mail Online, March 6, 2012. www.dailymail.co.uk/news/article-2110722/Rich-Chinese-thrill-seekers-paying-50-000-trip-lifetime--kill-endangered-polar-bears.html (accessed April 5, 2014).

8   G.A. Bradshaw, "Bear in Mind—15 Minutes of Shame—Art and Life in an Age of Double Speak," *Psychology Today,* March 13, 2012. www.psychologytoday.com/blog/bear-in-mind/201203/15-minutes-shame (accessed April 5, 2014).

9   Marc Bekoff and Jessica Pierce, *Wild Justice: The Moral Lives of Animals*, University of Chicago Press, 2009.

CHAPTER TWO

1   Jeanne Reimer, Proprietor, Churchill Wild, Seal River Heritage Lodge, personal communication, May 08, 2012, www.churchillwild.com (accessed April 5, 2014).
2   Tom Smith, Research Biologist, Brigham Young University, personal communication, July 16, 2012.
3   Christine Bartos, Curator of Ungulates and Small Mammals, Philadelphia Zoo, Pennsylvania, personal communication, July 11, 2012.
4   Imre Karacs, "Ursula and the Two Bears—Kenny and Boris Were Stars in East Germany, Says Imre Karacs, but with the State Circus Gone, Nobody Wants Them," *The Independent,* November 14, 1999. www.independent.co.uk/news/ursula-and-the-two-bears-1125911.html (accessed April 5, 2014).
5   Bruce Owen, "Polar Bears in Mexican Circus—Province of Manitoba—Activists Appalled," *Winnipeg Free Press,* March 29, 1996.
6   Kenneth Ekvall, Zoologist, Orso Bear Park, Sweden, personal communication, August 9, 2010.
7   Ryan De Voe, Senior Veterinarian, North Carolina Zoo, personal communication, July 23, 2012.

CHAPTER THREE

1   Jeff Owen, Animal Management Supervisor, North Carolina Zoological Park, personal communication, March 5, 2012.
2   Chris Zaluski and Palmer Holton, *A Life on Display,* film. vimeo.com/18069614 (2010; accessed January 20, 2014).
3   Owen.

4   Ibid.

5   Zoominfo.com. Robert H. Mattlin, Executive Director, Marine Mammal Commission, March 13, 2003. www.zoominfo.com/ p/Robert-Mattlin/129845271 (accessed January 20, 2014).

6   Leahy, April 27, 2012.

7   Ken Faulkner, "Treat It with Respect—In Puerto Rican Court, Detroit Zoo's Chief Vet Testifies in Animal Cruelty Case, *Habitat: The Detroit Zoological Society Journal* 15, no. 3 (2002).

8   Ibid.

9   Ann Duncan, Chief Veterinarian, Detroit Zoo and Belle Isle Nature Zoo, personal communication, May 16, 2012.

10   Diana Weinhardt, Northern Trail Supervisor, Minnesota Zoo, personal communication, February 17, 2012.

11   Ibid.

12   Holly Reed, Veterinarian, Point Defiance Zoo, Tacoma, Washington, personal communication, September 17, 2012.

13   Duncan.

14   Ibid.

CHAPTER FOUR

1   Jill Robinson, Founder, Animals Asia Foundation, personal communication, October 3, 2012.

CHAPTER FIVE

1   Debbie Leahy, personal communication, March 5, 2013.

2   Andrew E. Derocher, *Polar Bears: A Complete Guide to Their Biology and Behavior,* Johns Hopkins University Press, 2012.

3   Valeria Zamisch and Jennifer Vonk, "Spatial Memory in Captive American Black Bears (*Ursus Americanus*)," *Journal of Comparative Psychology* 126 (2012): 372–387.

4   Charles Russell, Bear Behaviorist, personal communication, February 12, 2013.

5   Henk Kiliaan, *The Possible Use of Tools by Polar Bears to Obtain Their Food,* 1974; reprinted from Norsk Polarinstitutt Årbok, 1972.

6   Ben Kilham, Bear Rehabilitator, personal communication, November 2012. www.benkilham.com/Benkilham.com/BEAR_BOOKS_AND_VIDEOS.html (accessed April 5, 2014).

CHAPTER SIX

1   Leahy, Personal Campaign Notes, People for the Ethical Treatment of Animals, 2002.
2   Jason Pratte, Animal Training Coordinator, Omaha Henry Doorly Zoo and Aquarium, personal communication, August 26, 2013.
3   Ibid.
4   Ian Stirling, Bear Biologist, University of Alberta, personal communication, March 28, 2013.

CHAPTER EIGHT

1   Tom Roy, Docent, Detroit Zoological Society, personal communication, July 12, 2013.

CHAPTER TEN

1   Ken and Sherri Gigliotti, personal communication, August 22, 2014.
2   Ibid.
3   Leahy, March 5, 2013.
4   Sarah Bexell, Director of Conservation Education and Communications, Chengdu Research Base of Giant Panda Breeding, personal communication. July 19, 2013.
5   BBC News/Europe, *Berlin Rallies Behind Baby Bear,* March 20, 2007. news.bbc.co.uk/2/hi/europe/6470509.stm (accessed January 21, 2014).
6   Ibid.
7   Ibid.
8   Jill Robinson, personal communication, August 12, 2013.
9   Ibid.
10 Ibid.
11 Timothy Appleby, "Harper Greets Pandas at Airport, Calling

Them 'National Treasures,'" *The Globe and Mail,* March 25, 2013.
www.theglobeandmail.com/news/toronto/harper-greets-pandas-at-airport-calling-them-national-treasures/article10279675/ (accessed
January 21, 2014).

12 Glenda Luymes, "Beyond Just Bears," *The Province,* October 16, 2012.
www.youtube.com/watch?v=sVdlvW8gRn4 (accessed April 5, 2014).

13 Karine Hauser and Anna Hauser, Co-Founders, Hauser Bears, personal
communication, August 26, 2013. hauserbears.com/ (accessed
January 21, 2014).

14 Scott Carter, Chief Life Sciences Officer, Detroit Zoological Society,
personal communication, May 17, 2013.

REFERENCES

CHAPTER ONE

Anonymous. Fur Canada. January 2014. Personal communication.

Environment Canada. November 10, 2011. "Species at Risk Act." News release. www.ec.gc.ca/default.asp?lang=En&n=714D9AAE-1&news=A7830770-FBE9-4FD7-8DD2-DCCB99B2DFD0 (accessed April 5, 2014).

Gamenews. December 5, 2013. "Polar Bear Hunting on Rise Despite Species' Decline." Press release. www.enewspf.com/latest-news/science science-a-environmental/48487-polar-bear-hunting-on-rise-despite-species-decline.html (accessed April 5, 2014).

Hailer, F. et al. 2012. "Nuclear Genomic Sequences Reveal That Polar Bears Are an Old and Distinct Bear Lineage." *Science* 336: 344–347.

Henton, D. February 22, 2012. "Wildlife Officers Shoot 145 Black Bears in Oilsands Region." *Calgary Herald*.

Ingólfsson, Ó., and Wiig, Ø. 2009. "Late Pleistocene Fossil Find in Svalbard— The Oldest Remains of a Polar Bear (*Ursus maritimus Phipps*, 1744) Ever Discovered." *Polar Research* 28: 455–462.

International Union for Conservation of Nature (IUCN) Polar Bear Specialist Group (PBSG). pbsg.npolar.no/en/status/ (accessed April 5, 2014).

Lindqvist, C. et al. 2010. *Complete Mitochondrial Genome of a Pleistocene Jawbone Unveils the Origin of Polar Bear.* Proceedings of the National Academy of Sciences 39: 15758–15763.

Miller, W. et al. 2012. *Polar and Brown Bear Genomes Reveal Ancient Admixture and Demographic Footprints of Past Climate Change.* Proceedings of the National Academy of Sciences. www.pnas.org/cgi/doi/10.1073/pnas.1210506109 (accessed April 5, 2014).

RIA Novosti. March 21, 2013. *Hundreds of Polar Bears Killed Annually in Russia—IFAW*. en.ria.ru/russia/20130321/180167887/Hundreds-of-Polar-Bears-Killed-Annually-in-Russia--IFAW.html (accessed April 5, 2014).

Simpson, P. March 6, 2012. "Rich Chinese Thrill Seekers Paying £50,000 for 'Trip of a Lifetime...' to Kill Endangered Polar Bears." *Mail Online*. www.dailymail.co.uk/news/article-2110722Rich-Chinese-thrill-seekers-paying-50-000-trip-lifetime--kill-endangered-polar-bears.html (accessed April 5, 2014).

Sokalov, V.E. 1982. *Mammal Skin*. University of California Press.

Stirling, I. 2011. *Polar Bears—A Natural History of a Threatened Species*. Fitzhenry & Whiteside.

Stirling, I. March 3, 2012. University of Alberta, Edmonton. Personal communication.

Stirling, I. et al. 2008. "Quantitative Support for a Subjective Fatness Index for Immobilized Polar Bears." *Journal of Wildlife Management* 72: 568–574.

United States Fish and Wildlife Service. 2014. "Species Profile, Polar Bear (*Ursus maritimus*)." ecos.fws.gov/speciesProfile/profile/speciesProfile.action?spcode=A0IJ (accessed April 5, 2014).

Vongraven, D. November 12, 2011. "Nunavut to Increase Harvest in Western Hudson Bay." International Union for Conservation of Nature (IUCN) Polar Bear Specialist Group PBSG. pbsg.npolar.no/en/news/archive/2011/WH-catch-Nunavut-2011.html (accessed April 5, 2014).

Weinhardt, D. February 17, 2012. Minnesota Zoo. Personal communication.

CHAPTER TWO

Anonymous. 2002. "Saving the Suarez Seven." *Animal Welfare Institute Quarterly* (51)2.

Bartos, C. July 11, 2012. Franklin Park Zoo, Massachusetts. Personal communication.

Belting, T. August 6, 2012. Seattle Aquarium. Personal communication.

Brandis, R. June 7, 2001. *United States Department of Agriculture* USDA. *Animal and Plant Health Inspection Service APHIS, Animal Care Inspection Report 94-C-0112.*

Circopedia—The Free Encyclopedia of the International Circus. www.circopedia.org/index.php/Ursula_B%C3%B6ttcher (accessed April 5, 2014).

Dyck, M.G., and Kebreab, E. 2009. "Estimating the Energetic Contribution of Polar Bear (*Ursus maritimus*) Summer Diets to the Total Energy Budget." *Journal of Mammalogy* (90)3: 585–593.

Environment Canada. November 10, 2011. "Canada's Environment Minister Declares Polar Bear Species of Concern." News release. www.ec.gc.ca/default.asp?lang=En&n=714D9AAE1&news=A7830770-FBE9-4FD7-8DD2-DCCB99B2DFD0 (accessed April 5, 2014).

Government of Canada. 1985. Convention on the International Trade of Endangered Species of Wild Fauna and Flora (CITES) Permit No. Man. 078.

Government of Canada. 1985. Convention on the International Trade of Endangered Species of Wild Fauna and Flora (CITES) Permit No. Man. 079.

Government of Manitoba. 1990. *The Endangered and Ecosystems Species Act,* C.C.S.M. c. E11. web2.gov.mb.ca/laws/statutes/ccsm/e111e.php (accessed April 5, 2014).

Government of Manitoba. 2002. *Polar Bear Protection Act,* C.C.S.M. c. P94. web2.gov.mb.ca/laws/statutes/ccsm/p094e.php (accessed April 5, 2014).

Government of Manitoba. 2010. *The Wildlife Act,* C.C.S.M. c. W130. web2.gov.mb.ca/laws/statutes/ccsm/w130e.php (accessed April 5, 2014).

Hedberg, G.E. 2002. "Polar Bears." In *Hand Rearing Wild and Domestic Mammals,* 181–190. Ed. L.J. Gage. Blackwell Publishing.

Hedberg, G.E. 2012. Registered veterinary technician. Personal communication.

Hedberg, G.E. et al. 2011. "Milk Composition in Free-Ranging Polar Bears (*Ursus maritimus*) as a Model for Captive Rearing Milk Formula." *Zoo Biology* (30)5: 550–565.

Herrero, S., and Fleck, S. 1990. "Injury to People Inflicted by Black, Grizzly or Polar Bears—Recent Trends and New Insights." *International Conference on Bear Research and Management* 8: 25–32.

Jonkel, C.J. March 26, 2012. Great Bear Foundation. Personal communication.

Jonkel, C.J. et al. 1972. "Further Notes on Polar Bear Denning." *International Conference on Bear Research and Management* 2: 142–158.

Karacs, I. November 14, 1999. "Ursula and the Two Bears—Kenny and Boris Were Stars in East Germany, Says Imre Karacs, but with the State Circus Gone, Nobody Wants Them." *The Independent.* www.independent.co.uk/news/ursula-and-the-two-bears-1125911.html (accessed April 5, 2014).

Laidlaw, R. 1997. *Manitoba's Forgotten Polar Bears—An Examination of Manitoba's Polar Bear Export Program.* Zoocheck Canada Inc. www.zoocheck.com/Reportpdfs/Manitoba%20Polar%20Bear%20Report.pdf (accessed April 5, 2014).

Middaugh, J.P. 1987. "Human Injury from Bear Attacks in Alaska, 1900–1985." *Alaska Medicine* 28: 121–126.

Owen, B. March 29, 1996. "Polar Bears in Mexican Circus—Province of Manitoba—Activists Appalled." *Winnipeg Free Press.*

Owen, B. March 29, 1996. "Crusade Seeks End to Polar Bear Trade." *Winnipeg Free Press.*

People for the Ethical Treatment of Animals (PETA). 2002. *Suarez Bro. Circus Polar Bear Discrepancies & Death Data Report, 2002.*

Reed, H. July 15, 2012. Point Defiance Zoo and Aquarium, Tacoma, Washington. Personal communication.

Roberts, A.M. 2002. "Polar Bears Suffer in the Suarez Brothers Circus." *Animal Welfare Institute Quarterly* 51(1).

Smith, T. et al. 2007. "Post-Den Emergence Behavior of Polar Bears (*Ursus maritimus*) in Northern Alaska." *Arctic* 60 (2): 187–194.

Stirling, I. 2011. *Polar Bears—A Natural History of a Threatened Species.* Fitzhenry & Whiteside.

Stirling, I., and McEwan, E.H. 1975. "The Caloric Value of Whole Ringed Seals (*Phoca hispida*) in Relation to Polar Bear (*Ursus maritimus*) Ecology and Hunting Behaviour." *Canadian Journal of Zoology* 53: 1021–1027.

United States Code. 1973. *Endangered Species Act, 50* CFR § 17.40(q). www.law.cornell.edu/uscode/16/usc_sup_01_16_10_35.html (accessed April 5, 2014).

United States Code. 2008. *Animal Welfare Act 1966,* as amended in 2008, 9 C.F.R. § 3.104(e). awic.nal.usda.gov (accessed April 5, 2014).

Watkins, W. April 26, 2012. Manitoba Conservation and Water Stewardship. Personal communication.

CHAPTER THREE

Duncan, A. May 16, 2012. Detroit Zoological Society. Personal communication.

Leahy, D. April 27, 2012. Humane Society of the United States. Personal communication.

Owen, J. March 5, 2012. North Carolina Zoological Park. Personal communication.

Sokalov, V.E. 1982. *Mammal Skin.* University of California Press.

Tabaka, C. March 15, 2013. World Chelonian Trust. Personal communication.

CHAPTER FOUR

Grandin, T. 1989. *Dendritic Growth in Somatosensory Region of Brain Cortex in Pigs Residing in a Simple or a Complex Environment.* Dissertation. Department of Animal Science, Colorado State University, University of Illinois.

Kessel, A., and Brent, L. 1995. *Behavioral Effects of Transferring Singly Housed Baboons to Outdoor Social Groups.* Proceedings of the Second International Conference on Environmental Enrichment. Copenhagen Zoo.

Poulsen, E.M.B. 1996. "Use of Fluoxetine for the Treatment of Stereotypical Pacing Behavior in a Captive Polar Bear." *Journal of the American Veterinary Medical Association* 209: 1470–1474.

CHAPTER FIVE

Cheek, R. 1997. *Learning to Talk Bear—So Bears Can Listen.* Skyline Publishing.

Kiliaan, H. 1974. *The Possible Use of Tools by Polar Bears to Obtain Their Food.* Reprint from Norsk Polarinstitutt Årbok, 1972.

Landriault, L.J. et al. 2000. "Nuisance Black Bears and What to Do with Them." Ontario Ministry of Natural Resources. www.mnr.gov.on.ca/stdprodconsume/groups/lr/@mnr/@bearwise/ documents/document/mnr_e000041.pdf (accessed April 5, 2014).

Sokalov, V.E. 1982. *Mammal Skin.* University of California Press.

Stirling, I. 2011. *Polar Bears—A Natural History of a Threatened Species.* Fitzhenry & Whiteside.

Weaver, K.M., and Pelton, M.T. 1994. "Denning Ecology of Black Bears in the Tensas River Basin of Louisiana." *International Conference of Bear Research and Management* 9: 427–433.

Zamisch, V., and Vonk, J. 2012. "Spatial Memory in Captive American Black Bears (*Ursus Americanus*)." *Journal of Comparative Psychology* 126: 372–387.

CHAPTER SIX

Ovsyanikov, N. 1996. *Polar Bears—Living with the White Bear.* Raincoast Books.

Poulsen, E. 2006. "Successful Captive Bear Introductions—Working with a Bear's Expectations." *International Bear News* 3: 15–16.

Stirling, I. 2011. *Polar Bears—A Natural History of a Threatened Species.* Fitzhenry & Whiteside.

CHAPTER EIGHT

Brooks, M. May 1, 2012. "Zoo Officials Announce Giant Step in Polar Bear Reproduction—Zoo Becomes First in the World to Attempt Artificial Insemination." News release. Monroe County Executive. www.senecaparkzoo.org/media/documents/Polar%20Bear%20AI%20 %285.1.12%29.pdf (accessed April 5, 2014).

China Watch. June 12, 2012. "Twin Bears Set Milestone." *The Shanghai Daily.* www.thechinawatch.com/2012/06/twin-bears-set-milestones (accessed April 5, 2014).

China's Satellite Launch Centers. November 17, 2005. "Sci-Tech Artificial Insemination Produces Twenty-Five Giant Pandas." Xinhua News

Agency. www.china.org.cn/english/scitech/149117.htm (accessed
April 5, 2014).
Cowan, P. February 13, 2013. "Zoo's Polar Bear Not Pregnant Following
Artificial Insemination—Zoo Is Committed to Further Understanding,
Attempting Polar Bear Conception." News release. Seneca Park Zoo.
www.senecaparkzoo.org/media/documents/FINAL%20-%20Polar%20
Bears%20(2.13.13).pdf (accessed April 5, 2014).

CHAPTER NINE

Derocher, A. et al. 2010. "Nursing Vocalization of a Polar Bear Cub." *Ursus,
International Association for Bear Research and Management* 2: 189–191.
Derocher, A., and Wiig, Ø. 1999. "Observation of Adoption in Polar Bears
(*Ursus maritimus*)," *Arctic* 4: 413–415.
Kozouz, R. April 12, 2005. "First Polar Bear Cub in over 15 Years Makes
Debut at the Detroit Zoo Tomorrow." PRNewswire.
www.thefreelibrary.com/First+Polar+Bear+Cub+in+Over+15+Years+
Makes+Debut+at+the+Detroit+Zoo...-a0131362551t+Polar+Bear+Cub+
in+Over+15+Years+Makes+Debut+at+the+Detroit+Zoo...-a0131362551
(accessed April 5, 2014).
Lunn, N.J. et al. 2000. "Cub Adoption by Polar Bears—Determining
Relatedness with Microsatellite Markers." *Journal of Zoology* 251: 23–30.
Olsen, H. January 2, 2011. *Polar Bear Cub Nursing.* Video. www.youtube.com/
watch?v=1ddrug5cEoA (accessed April 5, 2014).
Ovsyanikov, N. 1996. *Polar Bears: Living with the White Bear.* Raincoast Books.
Zoomin. TV Animals. January 7, 2013. *Live Birth of Polar Bear Twins at
Dierenrijk.* Video. www.youtube.com/watch?v=gdcEdmnsR6E (accessed
April 5, 2014).

CHAPTER TEN

Chicago Sun-Times.com. August 12, 2013. "Fayette County Man Mauled
by Captive Bear." Associated Press. www.suntimes.com/news/
nation/21888532-418/fayette-county-man-mauled-by-captive-
bear.html (accessed April 5, 2014).

Darwin Correspondence Project. University of Cambridge 2013. "Six Things Darwin Never Said - And One He Did." www.darwinproject.ac.uk/six-things-darwin-never-said (accessed April 5 2014).

DiGiacomo, J. October 5, 2009. "Pet Bear Kills Pennsylvania Woman." CNN.com. www.cnn.com/2009/US/10/05/bear.attack/index.html (accessed April 5, 2014).

GlobalPost.com. November 5, 2012. "Animal Trainer, Benjamin Cloutier, Mauled to Death by Grizzly Bears in Montana." www.globalpost.com/dispatch/news/regions/americas/united-states/121105/animal-trainer-benjamin-cloutier-mauled-death-gr (accessed April 5, 2014).

Government of British Columbia. November 19, 2013. Information Release FOI Request-FNR2013-00241. Open Information. www.openinfo.gov.bc.ca/ibc/search/detail.page?config=ibc&P110=recorduid:4824473&title=FOI Request-FNR-2013-00241 (accessed April 5, 2014).

IMDB.com. 1990–2014. *Midnight Sun (II)*, 2014. www.imdb.com/title/tt2390283/ (accessed April 5, 2014).

Kloss, H. 1974. "New Bear Exhibit in the West Berlin Zoo." *International Zoo Yearbook* 14: 223–225.

Linke, K. 2011. *2010 International Studbook for Polar Bears* (Ursus maritimus). World Association of Zoos and Aquaria (WAZA), Zoo Rostock.

Luymes, G. October 16, 2012. "Beyond Just Bears." *The Province.* www.youtube.com/watch?v=sVdlvW8gRn4 (accessed April 5, 2014).

McGrath, M. December 24, 2012. "Polar Bear Trade Ban Divides Campaigners." BBC News Science & Environment. www.bbc.co.uk/news/science-environment-20798136 (accessed April 5, 2014).

McGrath, M. March 7, 2013. "Polar Bear Trade Ban Vote Defeated at Meeting." BBC News Science & Environment. www.bbc.co.uk/news/science-environment-21703090 (accessed April 5, 2014).

National Oceanic and Atmospheric Administration. October 21, 1972. *Marine Mammal Protection Act* (MMPA). www.nmfs.noaa.gov/pr/laws/mmpa (accessed April 5, 2014).

Nissan Leaf. 2010. "The Making of Polar Bear Auto." *Daily Motion.*
www.dailymotion.com/video/xgj59d_nissan-leaf-the-making-of-
polar-bear_auto (accessed April 5, 2014).

Pringle, P. April 23, 2008. "Showbiz Grizzly Kills Trainer–Stuntman."
Los Angeles Times. articles.latimes.com/2008/apr/23/local/
me-bearattack23 (accessed April 5, 2014).

Sheeran, T.J. August 20, 2010. "Ohio Bear Owned by PETA Foe Kills Its
Caretaker." *The Washington Times.* www.washingtontimes.com/
news/2010/aug/20/ohio-bear-owned-peta-foe-kills-its-caretaker
(accessed April 5, 2014).

Superillu. "Ursula Böttcher– Mein Leben mit den Eisbären [My Life with
Polar Bears.]" www.superillu.de/exklusiv/ursula-boettcher-mein-
leben-mit-den-eisbaeren-die-beruehmte-dompteurin-im-interview
(accessed April 5, 2014).

Tieg, A. May 31, 2013 "Monkey Business–Eccentric Berlin Zoo Director
under Scrutiny." Spiegel Online International. www.spiegel.de/
international/germany/lawyers-investigate-leadership-of-berlin-zoo-
director-blaszkiewitz-a-902790.html (accessed April 5, 2014).

United States Department of Agriculture. July 27, 2011. Inspection
Report, License #34-C-0297. www.humanesociety.org/assets/pdfs/
wildlife/captive/captive-bear-incidents.PDF (accessed April 5, 2014).

Verband Deutscher Zoodirektoren. www.zoodirektoren.de/ (accessed
April 5, 2014).

World News on NBCNews.com. February 17, 2013. "Popular Polar Bear Knut
Becomes Museum Display." worldnews.nbcnews.com/_news/2013/
02/17/16993284-popular-polar-bear-knut-becomes-museum-
display?lite (accessed April 5, 2014).

INDEX

223

ELSE POULSEN is an award-winning zookeeper with over twenty-five years of experience working with captive and wild bears. She is internationally recognized as a bear behavior expert and has worked at the Calgary and Detroit zoos, among other institutions. She holds a BSc in biological sciences and a diploma in zookeeping. Poulsen works around the globe as an animal management consultant for zoos, sanctuaries, and wildlife rehabilitators and is an accomplished author and public speaker. She lives in Ontario, Canada.